Elements of Music

Third Edition

Handwritten notes:

+ scale degree #s, names, transposition, key signatures, alto clef

Test 2: Do exercises from
Week (Lec) 4 - Jan 29
↳ lessons 9-13
Lec 5: major scales &
circle of fifths
(lessons 14-16)
Lec 6: minor scales
(lessons 17-20)
+ supplementary

Joseph N. Straus
The Graduate Center
The City University of New York

PEARSON

Boston   Columbus   Indianapolis   New York   San Francisco   Upper Saddle River
Amsterdam   Cape Town   Dubai   London   Madrid   Milan   Munich   Paris   Montreal   Toronto
Delhi   Mexico City   São Paulo   Sydney   Hong Kong   Seoul   Singapore   Taipei   Tokyo

Editorial Director: *Craig Campanella*
Editor in Chief: *Sarah Touborg*
Executive Editor: *Richard Carlin*
Editorial Assistant: *Lily Norton*
Vice President Director of Marketing: *Brandy Dawson*
Executive Marketing Manager: *Kate Stewart Mitchell*
Marketing Assistant: *Lisa Kirlick*
Managing Editor: *Melissa Feimer*
Project Manager: *Marlene Gassler*
Senior Manufacturing Manager: *Mary Fischer*
Senior Operations Specialist: *Brian Mackey*

Creative Director, Cover: *Jayne Conte*
Cover Designer: *Bruce Kenselaar*
Cover Photo Credit: *Orla/ Shutterstock*
Senior Media Editor: *David Alick*
Media Project Manager: *Rich Barnes*
Full-Service Project Management: *Emily Bush,*
S4Carlisle Publishing Services
Composition: *S4Carlisle Publishing Services*
Printer/Binder: *LSC Communications*
Printer/ Insert: *LSC Communications*
Cover Printer: *LSC Communications*

Copyright © 2012, 2008, 2003 by Joseph N. Straus

Library of Congress Cataloging-in-Publication Data
Straus, Joseph Nathan.
  Elements of music / Joseph N. Straus. —3rd ed.
      p. cm.
  ISBN-13: 978-0-205-00709-7
  ISBN-10: 0-205-00709-0
  1. Music theory.   I. Title.
  MT6.S788E44 2012
  781.2—dc22   2011006152

12 17

www.pearsonhighered.com

ISBN 10:   0-205-00709-0
ISBN 13: 978-0-205-00709-7
Exam Copy ISBN 10:   0-205-20503-8
Exam Copy ISBN 13: 978-0-205-20503-5

Contents

Preface

Who is this book for?

This book is designed for a one-semester course for two groups of students: (1) Nonmusic majors who are taking a course in music because they want to write their own music or are simply curious about how music is put together; (2) Aspiring music majors who need some extra work in fundamental topics before beginning a sequence of theory courses for music majors.

What topics does this book cover?

This book covers the traditional fundamental topics in tonal music theory: pitch notation in bass and treble clefs; rhythm and meter; major and minor scales; intervals; triads and seventh chords; simple harmonic progressions and cadences. These topics are relevant to a broad range of tonal styles, including classical music in the Western tradition from roughly 1600 to 1900 and more recent jazz and popular music.

What makes this book different?

1. **Musical literature.** This book is immersed in musical literature. It includes an anthology of core works in diverse tonal styles (both in score and recorded on CD), and these are the source of all of the musical examples and many of the written exercises. Each musical excerpt is thus understood in its larger context; there are no isolated snippets. The theoretical concepts and musical works are integrated with each other. As students learn each basic concept, they see how it functions in music of high artistic quality. At the same time, they use their newly acquired theoretical ability to come to an intimate understanding of a small group of fine works. They learn the concepts through the musical works, and the musical works through the concepts.

2. **Interactivity.** Virtually all of the homework exercises in this book are available in *Finale*, the top music notation software program. By doing the exercises online at a computer instead of with paper and pencil, students will be able to hear the music they are studying and to hear what they have written. Exercises that are available in *Finale* are identified in the text by this symbol:

3. **Flexibility.** The book is organized into six chapters: (1) pitch; (2) rhythm and meter; (3) scales; (4) intervals; (5) triads and seventh chords; and (6) harmony. This transparent organization provides instructors with a significant degree of flexibility. For example, teachers who prefer to teach rhythm before, or simultaneously with, early work in pitch notation will find it easy to do so. The book, with its extensive, imaginative, interactive exercises, is designed as a set of flexible resources for the teacher rather than a prescribed curricular sequence that must be followed in lockstep. The main topics can be easily located either in the Table of Contents at the beginning of the book or in the extensive Glossary at the end.

4. **Written exercises and assignments.** For each concept, there are extensive written exercises, both in traditional written and electronic (*Finale*) formats. Many of the exercises incorporate music from the anthology and many encourage creative composition. There are far more exercises than any one class could do; the instructor will thus have a wide range of choices. Many of the exercises also work well for in-class drill and study. At the end of the first five chapters, you will find a Self-Test (with answers provided on subsequent pages).

5. **In-class activities.** Each lesson is accompanied by suggested in-class activities, including singing, dictation, and keyboard exercises. These activities do not comprise a course in sight-singing, dictation, or keyboard harmony; rather, they are designed to supplement and reinforce the theory lessons. The goal of these activities, and of the book as a whole, is to bring beginning students into close, intimate contact with musical materials, not only to understand them intellectually but to embody them in some way. At every stage, this book emphasizes that music is to be heard and made, not merely seen and contemplated in the abstract.

What resources are available on the Web?

To download the homework exercises written in *Finale*, go to www.mysearchlab.com.

You will also find a link to *Finale*, where you can purchase *Finale NotePad* directly from the company (the current price is less than $10). With this software, you will be able to do virtually all of the exercises at your computer, hearing what you are doing as you do it. Then print out a beautiful, clean copy to hand in, or email it to your instructor, as directed.

Acknowledgments

At an early stage in writing the first edition of this book, I benefited immensely from advice offered by a large number of colleagues and friends around the country: Mark Anson-Cartwright (Queens College, CUNY), Larry Arnold (University of North Carolina at Pembroke), Joseph Auner (Tufts University), Jean Aydelotte (University of Texas at Austin), James Baker (Brown University), Amy Bauer (University of California at Irvine), Candace Brower (Northwestern University), Steven Bruns (University of Colorado at Boulder), Poundie Burstein (Hunter College, CUNY), Eleanor Cory (Queensborough Community College, CUNY), John Covach (Eastman School of Music), Walter Everett (University of Michigan at Ann Arbor), Yayoi Everett (Emory University), Cynthia Folio (Temple University), Deborah Freedman (Missouri Western State College), Daniel Harrison (Yale University), Patricia Helm (Colby College), Richard Hermann (University of New Mexico), Sara Holtzschue (Queensborough Community College, CUNY), William Horne (Loyola University), Peter Kaminsky (University of Connecticut at Storrs), Gary Karpinski (University of Massachusetts at Amherst), Stefan Kostka (University of Texas at Austin), Joseph Kraus (University of Nebraska at Lincoln), Philip Lambert (Baruch College, City University of New York), Steve Larson (University of Oregon at Portland), Stephan Lindemann (Brigham Young University), John Link (William Paterson College), Justin London (Carleton College), Elizabeth Marvin (Eastman School of Music), William Marvin (Oberlin Conservatory), John McCann (Tufts University), Jairo Moreno (New York University), Akane Mori (Hartt School of Music), Shaugn O'Donnell (City College, CUNY), Jeffrey Perry (Louisiana State University), Mark Rimple (West Chester College), Lynne Rogers (William Paterson College), Michael Rogers (University of Oklahoma at Norman), Dean Roush (Wichita State University), Philip Rupprecht (Duke University), Matthew Santa (Texas Tech University), Janet Schmalfeldt (Tufts University), Stephen Slottow (University of North Texas at Denton), David Smyth (Louisiana State University), James Sobaskie (Hofstra University), Deborah Stein (New England Conservatory), Gary Sudano (Purdue University), Kristin Wendland (Emory University), and Norman Wick (Southern Methodist University).

As the book took shape, I received additional guidance from Ellie Hisama, Shaugn O'Donnell, and Matthew Santa, as well as from the following reviewers: Kurt Ellenberger, Grand Valley State University; Joann Feldman, Sonoma State University; Ann Usher, University of Akron; Daniel McCarthy, University of Akron; Roger Letson, De Anza College; Michael Kallstrom, Western Kentucky University; Matthew Shaftel, Florida State University; Leslie Odom, University of Florida; Matthew Santa, Texas Tech University; and Gene Trantham, Bowling Green State University. When the book was in draft, four colleagues graciously offered to field-test it with their students: Robert Bowen (West Chester University), Chandler Carter (Hofstra University), Deborah Thoreson (Emory University), and Gene Trantham (Bowling Green State University). This was extremely helpful to me, as was the advice offered by several classes of my own students at Queens College (especially Michael Brooks). Hedi Siegel provided a fine translation of the text for the song by Josephine Lang. I received valuable editorial assistance from Michael Molloy and Michael Berry.

In preparing the second edition of this book, a number of colleagues offered valuable advice based on their experience with the first edition: Michael Buchler, Pat Hall, Heather Laurel, Luiz Lopes, Eve Poudrier, Matthew Santa, Margaret Thomas, Anton Vishio, and James Webster. Six reviewers engaged by Pearson made valuable suggestions for revision: Pam Davis (Bowling Green State University), Roger Letson (DeAnza College), Adam Ricci (UNC Greensboro), Michael Kallstrom (Western Kentucky University), Leslie Odom (University of Florida), and Don Traut (UNC Greensboro). *Finale* files of the exercises were prepared by Mario Mazzoli and Thomas Robinson. At Pearson, Richard Carlin took over where Chris Johnson left off and saw the work into print. I was fortunate to have Debra Nichols as the skilled copyeditor for this book, and I received valuable editorial assistance from Patty Howland, Ryan Jones, and Eve Poudrier.

In preparing the third edition, I once again had the benefit of advice from experienced colleagues, especially Roxane Prevost and Sylvia Kahan. I am grateful for the reviews of the proposed changes by Brian Allison of Collin County Community College, Mary Ann Bogar of Middlesex County College, Jayne Campbell of Glendale College, Byron Delto of Glendale College, Reed Hoyt of the University at Albany, Michael Kurek of Vanderbilt University, Shafer Mahoney of Hunter College CUNY, Mark McConnell of Crafton Hills College, Jocelyn Neal of the University of North Carolina at Chapel Hill, Matthew Schildt of Adams State College, Homer Stewart of Howard College, James Webster of Cornell University, Kristin Wendland of Emory University, and Mark Zanter of Marshall University. Pedro Segarra assisted in the preparation of the musical examples, and in other valuable ways. Once again, I was fortunate to have the guidance of Richard Carlin, Music Editor at Pearson as well as the rest of Pearson's superb editorial team.

As always, my deepest debt of gratitude is owed to Sally Goldfarb, my peerless partner.

What's new in this third edition?

- Enhanced layout, with critical terms set in boldface in the text and highlighted in blue in the book's margins.

- Exercises available online in *Finale*. Students can do their exercises on their computers, using *Finale*, the top music notation software. They will be able to hear the music they are writing as they write it.

What resources are available for teachers?

In addition to the clear explanations in the text and the profusion of in-class activities and exercises (including the availability online of the exercises written in *Finale*), instructors may wish to download the Teacher's Manual. This manual, available through the Pearson website www.pearsonhighered.com, contains suggested syllabi for a course on music fundamentals as well as answers for all of the exercises in the book.

What is the goal of this book?

Learning music is like learning a foreign language. Some hard work is required to master the basic grammar and vocabulary. But once you gain a reasonable degree of fluency, a whole new world opens up to you. You can express yourself and communicate in a new language, and you can listen with far deeper understanding when others speak to you. Mastery of the basic material of music described in this book will enable you to write your own music in a more thoughtful way, enable you to talk with and learn from other musicians, and give you insight into the uses that master composers have made of these basic materials. A great adventure lies ahead of you in the following pages!

1 Pitch

Lesson 1: Staff

In this lesson you will learn about the five-line staff, pitches and notes, noteheads, ascending and descending motion, steps and leaps, and ledger lines.

Music is written on a five-line **staff:** five parallel lines separated by four spaces. **Staff**

Five-line staff

Fifth line
Fourth line
Third line
Second line
First line

Fourth space
Third space
Second space
First space

A **pitch** is a musical sound at some particular point along the continuum from the lowest to the highest audible sound. A pitch is written as a **note** placed either on a line or in a space on the five-line staff. A **notehead**, which specifies where on the staff a note is to occur, is an oval shape that may be either open or filled in.

Pitch
Note
Notehead

Open noteheads   Filled-in noteheads
on a line   in a space   on a line   in a space

Noteheads

Use the staves that follow to practice writing noteheads. They should be oval (not round) in shape and tilted to the right. Noteheads in a space should just touch the lines above and below; noteheads on a line should fill half the spaces above and below.

Too small   Too big   Wrong shape   Just right

Write fifteen filled-in noteheads on the lines and spaces of this staff.

Writing
noteheads

Write fifteen open noteheads on the lines and spaces of this staff.

To move from a note to a **higher-sounding** note, you **ascend** on the staff. To move from a note to a **lower-sounding** note, you **descend**.

High/Ascend
Low/Descend

Ascending
and descending

Step
Leap

There are two kinds of melodic motion: by **step** and by **leap** (also some-times called a skip). A step involves motion from a line up or down to an adjacent space, or from a space up or down to an adjacent line. A leap is any motion bigger than a step. Steps and leaps may be either ascending or descending.

Steps
and leaps

Ledger line

For notes that lie above or below the staff, the staff may be temporarily extended by **ledger lines**. These lines function and are spaced just like the lines of the staff, but begin just before an individual notehead and end just after it.

Ledger lines

Use the staff that follows to practice writing noteheads with ledger lines. Notes in the spaces above the staff need ledger lines below (not above) them; notes in the spaces below the staff need ledger lines above (not below) them.

Writing
ledger
lines

Use ledger lines to write notes above the staff.

Use ledger lines to write notes below the staff.

Lesson 1: In-class activities

1. Singing. The instructor will play or sing a note. Sing the note you hear.

2. Dictation. The instructor will play two notes in succession. Identify the melodic motion as ascending or descending, step or leap. Sing the notes.

3. Dictation. The instructor will play three notes in succession. Identify the melodic motion as: (1) low-middle-high; (2) low-high-middle; (3) middle-low-high; (4) middle-high-low; (5) high-low-middle; (6) high-middle-low. Sing the notes.

Name: _____

Date: _____

Instructor's Name: _____

LESSON 1: EXERCISES

Note: In the Exercises in this chapter, and in every chapter of this book, you will confront fully notated musical excerpts, replete with symbols of all kinds, including many you will not be learning about until later: clef signs, key signatures, time signatures, stems, and beams, among others. The number and variety of the symbols can be confusing at first. For now, just focus on the filled-in or open noteheads and ignore any unfamiliar symbols.

1-1. In these melodies, identify each motion as an ascending step (AS), descending step (DS), ascending leap (AL), or descending leap (DL). Ignore any unfamiliar notational symbols and focus only on the noteheads. Remember that a step involves motion on the staff from a line to the adjacent space, or vice versa. A leap is any motion bigger than a step.

a. Arlen, "Over the Rainbow" (the first three notes of the melody describe a melodic shape that occurs two more times).

b. Rodríguez, "La Cumparsita" (the melody involves a contrast between leaps and steps).

c. Haydn, String Quartet (the descending leaps get bigger and bigger).

d. Mozart, "Dove sono" (the melody begins mostly with steps and ends mostly with small leaps).

e. Bach, Fugue in G minor (the leap in the middle is flanked by steps before and after).

f. Lang, Song (leaps at the beginning are balanced by steps at the end).

g. Ellington, "It Don't Mean a Thing" (the melody consists mostly of small leaps).

h. Mendelssohn, Piano Trio (the leaps are usually followed by steps).

mysearchlab

1-2. Write ascending or descending steps or leaps. Remember that a step involves motion on the staff from a line to the adjacent space, or vice versa. A leap is any motion bigger than a step.

a. Write an ascending step above each of these notes.

Name: _____

Date: _____

Instructor's Name: _____

b. Write an ascending leap above each of these notes.

c. Write a descending step below each of these notes.

d. Write a descending leap below each of these notes.

Lesson 2: Keyboard

In this lesson you will learn about the piano keyboard, black and white keys, letter names for notes, steps and leaps, octaves, and piano fingering.

In learning basic musical concepts, it is often useful to refer to the **piano keyboard**. The typical piano keyboard contains eighty-eight **keys**, some **black** and some **white**, each producing a different pitch. Moving toward the right, the pitches get higher; moving toward the left, the pitches get lower.

Piano keyboard
Black keys
White keys

Piano keyboard

We will focus for now just on the white keys. Each white key has a **letter name**—one of the first seven letters of the alphabet: A, B, C, D, E, F, G. The asymmetrical layout of the black keys (alternating groups of two and three) provides each of the seven different white keys with a distinctive location. C, for example, is always found just below the group of two black keys. The C right in the middle of the keyboard is known as **middle C**.

Letter name

Middle C

Letter names

C D E F G A B C D E F G A B C D E F G A B C D E F G A B C

middle C

Moving from any white key to the adjacent white key, up or down, is a **step**. Each step takes you from one letter of the alphabet to the next. When you get up to G, you start over again on A. And, going the other direction, when you get down to A, you start over again on G.

Step

Steps

C D E F G A B C D E F G A B

Most of the adjacent white keys have a black key between them (C–D, D–E, F–G, G–A, and A–B). However, there is no black key between E and F or between B and C. We thus have two different sizes of step: The smaller **Half step** steps (where no black key intervenes) are called **half steps** and the larger steps (where there is a black key between two adjacent white keys) are called **Whole step** **whole steps.**

Leap   Moving from any white key to a nonadjacent white key is a **leap**. If you start on any key and leap up or down seven steps, you end up on another key with the same letter name. Seven steps span eight white keys and comprise an **Octave** **octave**. Pitches related by one or more octaves share the same name because they sound so much alike.

Octaves

In playing the piano, it is customary to refer to your fingers by number: the thumb is the first finger; the index finger is the second finger, and so on.

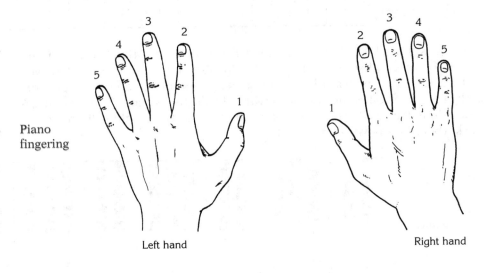

Piano fingering

Left hand   Right hand

Lesson 2: In-class activities

1. **Singing.** The instructor will play a note. Sing the note you hear, and then sing the note an octave higher or lower, as requested.

2. **Singing.** The instructor will play two white notes slowly in succession. Sing the notes, then identify them as an ascending or descending step or leap.

3. **Reciting.** Recite the letter names of the notes, ascending and descending, as follows (working for speed and accuracy):

   a. ascending: A–B–C–D–E–F–G–A—B–C–D–E–F–G–A–B—
      C–D–E–F–G–A–B–C—D–E–F–G–A–B–C–D—E–F–G–A–B–C–D–E—
      F–G–A–B–C–D–E–F—G–A–B–C–D–E–F–G

   b. descending: A–G–F–E–D–C–B–A—G–F–E–D–C–B–A–G—
      F–E–D–C–B–A–G–F—E–D–C–B–A–G–F–E—D–C–B–A–G–F–E–D—
      C–B–A–G–F–E–D–C—B–A–G–F–E–D–C–B

4. **Dictation.** The instructor will play two white notes slowly in succession. Identify the interval as either an octave or not-an-octave.

5. **Playing.** The instructor will play a white note near the middle of the keyboard. Play the note you hear.

6. **Playing.** The instructor will call out a letter name (A through G). Play the requested note, then the note a step above or below, then the note an octave above or below (as instructed—white notes only).

7. **Playing.** Using the thumb of your right hand, play any white note. Then play four ascending steps (fingering: 1-2-3-4-5) and return to the starting point (fingering: 5-4-3-2-1). Using the thumb of your left hand, play any white note. Then play four descending steps (fingering: 1-2-3-4-5) and return to the starting point (fingering: 5-4-3-2-1). Say the names of the notes as you play.

8. **Playing.** Using either hand, play any white note, then play as follows: octave up, step down, octave down, step down, octave up, step down, and so on. Use fingers 1 and 5 only. Name the notes as you play. Then begin again on any note, now playing as follows: octave down, step up, octave up, step up, octave down, step up, and so on. Again, use fingers 1 and 5 only and name the notes as you play.

Name: _____

Date: _____

Instructor's Name: _____

LESSON 2: EXERCISES

2-1. Identify the indicated keys by writing their letter names.

a.

All Cs and Fs

b.

All Bs and Gs

c.

All As and Ds

d.

All Bs and Es

e.

All Cs and Gs

2-2. Provide the letter name for each indicated key.

a.

C   E   G   C D   F   A

b.

D E   G   C D   F   B

c.

C ___ F ___ A B ___ ___ ___ ___ ___

d.

___ ___   ___ ___ ___ ___ ___

e.

___   ___   ___   ___   ___   ___   ___

2-3. Use arrows to indicate motions (white keys only). Remember that a step involves motion from one key to an adjacent key. An octave involves seven steps, up or down, and spans eight keys. Notes an octave apart have the same letter name.

a.

Step above

b.

Step below

c.

Octave above

d.

Octave above

e.

Octave below

Lesson 3: Treble clef

In this lesson you will learn about the treble clef, accidentals (sharp, flat, natural), semitones, and enharmonic equivalence.

A **clef** is used to identify locations on the staff with specific pitches. The most commonly used clef is the **treble clef**. This symbol, which is derived from a fancy, script G, is also called the **G clef**. It assigns the G above middle C to the second line of the staff. All of the remaining pitches are assigned to the other lines and spaces of the staff.

Clef
Treble clef
G clef

Treble clef

A B C D E F G A B C D E F G A B C D E
(middle C)

Use the staff that follows to practice writing the treble clef. You should write it in one continuous curve. The top of the clef extends just above the staff and the bottom extends just below it. The middle part of the clef circles around the G above middle C.

Trace these treble clefs.   Write ten treble clefs.

To name the black notes of the keyboard, we have to use **accidentals**—namely, a **sharp sign** (♯) which raises a note one **semitone** and a **flat sign** (♭), which lowers a note one semitone. A semitone is the smallest musical distance. From any key on the keyboard to the nearest adjacent key is a semitone. The black key that lies right between the white notes C and D, for example, can be called either C♯ (because it lies a semitone above C) or D♭ (because it lies a semitone below D). Because C♯ and D♭ refer to the same pitch, they are said to be **enharmonic equivalents**. On the staff, the accidental is written before the note, but when you say the name of the note, the accidental comes after, as in "C sharp" and "D flat."

Accidentals
Sharp
Semitone
Flat

Enharmonic equivalents

Enharmonic equivalents

C♯ / D♭   D♯ / E♭   F♯ / G♭   G♯ / A♭   A♯ / B♭

Natural   A note that is neither sharp nor flat is **natural** (♮). The white notes on the keyboard are thus C♮, D♮, E♮, F♮, G♮, A♮, and B♮.

The use of sharp and flat signs is not limited to naming the black notes of the keyboard. A sharp sign raises any note by one semitone and a flat sign lowers any note by one semitone. C♭, for example, is the note a semitone below C, so C♭ is enharmonically equivalent to B. Similarly, E♯ is the note a semitone above E, so E♯ and F are enharmonic equivalents.

Enharmonic equivalents

It may seem cumbersome or redundant to have different names for the same pitch. The reason has to do with the musical context in which the pitch occurs. Within one scale or harmony, for example, a given pitch might sound and act like a C♯, whereas in a different scale or harmony, the same pitch might sound and act like a D♭. A full discussion of this matter will have to wait until you know more about scales and harmonies, but the ability to confer different meanings on a single pitch is a wonderful musical resource.

Use the staves that follow to practice writing accidentals. In a flat sign, the vertical line is about two spaces long. The curved portion extends to the right and is aligned horizontally with the note it modifies.

Write flat signs in front of these notes.

In a sharp sign, the two vertical lines are about three spaces long and the two horizontal lines are angled slightly upward. Like the flat sign, the sharp sign is aligned with the note it modifies.

Write sharp signs in front of these notes.

In the natural sign, the vertical lines are about two spaces long and the two horizontal lines are angled slightly upward. Like all accidentals, the natural sign is aligned with the note it modifies.

Write natural signs in front of these notes.

Lesson 3: In-class activities

1. **Note reading.** Using Exercises 3-1, 3-2, and 3-3, speak the names of the notes as accurately, steadily, and quickly as you can.

2. **Singing.** The instructor will play or sing each of the following melodic fragments. Sing them back, holding each note for about one second and singing the letter name for each note. Sing an octave lower if that is more comfortable.

3. **Singing.** The instructor will play or sing each of the following melodic fragments, all highly simplified versions of melodies from the anthology. Sing them back, holding each note for about one second and singing the letter name for each note. Sing an octave lower if that is more comfortable.

4. **Dictation.** Within each group, the instructor will play all three melodies in order, then will play them again, one at a time, in a random order. Identify the fragment you hear and sing it back. Sing the letter name for each note.

5. Playing. Play the following sequences of notes with your right hand, using the fingering provided. Play each note for approximately one second. Say the name of the note as you play.

Name: _____

Date: _____

Instructor's Name: _____

LESSON 3: EXERCISES

3-1. Provide letter names for these notes on the treble staff (C, E, and G only). Work as quickly as you can.

3-2. Provide letter names for these notes (C, D, E, F, G, A, and B only). Work as quickly as you can.

mysearchlab

3-3. Provide letter names for these notes, including accidentals. (Ignore any unfamiliar symbols and just concentrate on naming the notes.)

a. Mozart, Piano Sonata (the melodic motion is primarily stepwise).

b. Bach, Chorale melody (the melody is in six parts, called *phrases*. The end of each phrase is identified with a symbol called a *fermata*, which indicates that a note is to be sustained for an indefinite duration.)

c. Haydn, String Quartet (this melody is divided roughly into two halves that begin the same way but end differently).

Name: _____

Date: _____

Instructor's Name: _____

    d. Bach, Fugue in G Major (the melody ascends slowly to its highpoint, then descends rapidly back to where it began).

    e. Handy, "St. Louis Blues" (the two halves of this melody begin differently but end the same).

    f. Schubert, "Heidenröslein" (the entire melody lies within one octave, from the G above middle C to the G an octave higher).

g. Mozart, "Dove sono" (the two phrases of this melody are shaped like arches, rising to a high point and then descending to their close).

3-4. Write the indicated notes on the treble staff.

Name: _____

Date: _____

Instructor's Name: _____

3-5. Use arrows to connect each note on the staff to the corresponding key on the keyboard. Your arrows should extend all the way to the proper key and they may not cross.

3-6. For each indicated key on the keyboard, write the corresponding note on the treble staff. You will need ledger lines for some of the higher-sounding notes.

b.

c.

3-7. Provide enharmonic notes. Remember that enharmonic notes share the same pitch, but have different letter names.

C# = Db   Eb = D#   A# = Bb   Cb = B   D# = Eb   F# = Gb   Fb = E

a.

G# =   Gb =   Bb =   Db =   Ab =   B =   E =

b.

Lesson 4: Bass clef

In this lesson you will learn about the bass clef, accidentals (sharp, flat, natural), and semitones.

Like the treble clef, the **bass clef** is used to assign pitches to specific places on the staff. Notes written in bass clef are usually lower in pitch than notes written in treble clef. The bass clef is sometimes called an **F clef** because its design is derived from a stylized letter F. It assigns the F below middle C to the fourth line of the staff. All of the remaining pitches are assigned to the other lines and spaces of the staff.

Bass clef

F clef vs Treble is Gclef! (handwritten)

As with the treble clef, the black keys are named using **accidentals** (sharps and flats) that raise or lower any note by one **semitone**.

Accidentals
Semitones

Use the staff that follows to practice writing the bass clef. The curve of the clef centers on the fourth line of the staff and the two dots surround it—one in the space above and one in the space below.

Trace these bass clefs.   Write ten bass clefs.

Lesson 4: In-class activities

1. **Note reading.** Using Exercises 4-1, 4-2, and 4-3, speak the names of the notes as accurately, steadily, and quickly as you can.

2. **Singing.** The instructor will play or sing each of the following melodic fragments. Sing them back, holding each note for about one second and singing the letter name for each note. Sing an octave higher if that is more comfortable.

3. Singing. The instructor will play or sing each of the following melodic fragments, all highly simplified versions of melodies from the anthology. Sing them back, holding each note for about one second and singing the letter name for each note. Sing an octave higher if that is more comfortable.

4. Dictation. Within each group, the instructor will play all three melodies in order, then will play them again, one at a time, in a random order. Identify the fragment you hear and sing it back. Sing the letter name for each note.

5. Playing. Play the following sequences of notes with your left hand, using the fingering provided. Play each note for approximately one second. Say the name of the note as you play.

Name: _____

Date: _____

Instructor's Name: _____

LESSON 4: EXERCISES

4-1. Provide letter names for these notes on the bass staff (C, E, and G only). Work as quickly as you can.

4-2. Provide letter names for these notes on the bass staff (C, D, E, F, G, A, and B only). Work as quickly as you can.

4-3. Provide letter names for these notes, including accidentals. (Ignore any unfamiliar symbols and just concentrate on naming the notes.)

a. Bach, Fugue in G minor (the melody pushes up to middle C from the C an octave below).

b. Chopin, Prelude in C minor (each note is heard simultaneously in two different octaves).

c. Mendelssohn, Piano Trio (the space outlined by the initial leap is filled in again and again).

d. Bach, Fugue in G Major (this melody moves mostly by step, but contains two large ascending leaps).

Name: _____

Date: _____

Instructor's Name: _____

e. Mozart, Piano Sonata (this bass line moves around quite a bit, but always returns to A).

f. Bach, Chorale melody (the first, third, and last phrases end on D).

g. Schubert, "Death and the Maiden" (this slow, stately bass line is designed to suggest the irresistibility of death and its fixity of purpose).

h. Lang, Song (this bass line starts and ends on E♭).

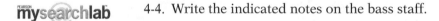

mysearchlab   4-4. Write the indicated notes on the bass staff.

4-5. Use arrows to connect each note on the staff to the corresponding key on the keyboard. Your arrows should extend all the way to the proper key and they may not cross.

Name: _____

Date: _____

Instructor's Name: _____

c.

4-6. For each indicated key on the keyboard, write the corresponding note on the bass staff. You will need ledger lines for some of the lower-sounding notes.

a.

b.

c.

Lesson 5: Great staff

In this lesson you will learn about the great staff.

Often music is written using two staves at the same time, with the higher notes written in treble clef and the lower notes in bass clef. The two staves are connected by a vertical line and a large brace. That combination, called the **great** **Great staff** **staff** (or **grand staff**), enables us to notate any pitch.

Great staff

middle C

    Notice that the two staves of the great staff can overlap to some extent. Middle C and the notes near it can be easily accommodated either in treble or in bass clef.

    The clef you use will depend on convenience and continuity—for example, if you are writing a melody in treble clef, and it dips below the staff, you will most likely continue writing in treble clef, with ledger lines, rather than jumping to bass clef.

Lesson 5: In-class activities

1. **Note reading.** Using Exercises 5-1, 5-2, and 5-3, speak the names of the notes as accurately, steadily, and quickly as you can.

2. **Singing.** The instructor will play or sing each of the following melodic fragments. Sing them back, holding each note for about one second and singing the letter name for each note.

3. Singing (duets). Divide into pairs or groups to sing the following duets. Hold each note for about one second and sing the letter name for each note.

4. Dictation. Within each group, the instructor will play all three duets in order, then will play them again, one at a time, in a random order. Identify the duet you hear and sing back the upper or lower part, as requested by your instructor. Sing the letter name for each note as you sing it.

5. Playing. Play the following sequences of notes with both hands together. Use the fingering provided. Play each note for about one second.

Name: _____

Date: _____

Instructor's Name: _____

LESSON 5: EXERCISES

5-1. Provide letter names for these notes on the great staff (C, E, and G only). Work as quickly as you can.

5-2. Provide letter names for these notes (C, D, E, F, G, A, and B only). Work as quickly as you can.

5-3. Provide letter names for these notes, including accidentals. For the notes in treble clef, write your answer above the staff; for the notes in bass clef, write your answer below the staff.

a. Haydn, String Quartet (these are the violin and cello melodies).

Name: _____

Date: _____

Instructor's Name: _____

    b. Chopin, Prelude in A Major (the melody in the treble clef, played by
        the pianist's right hand, is relatively active; the melody in the bass
        clef, played by the pianist's left hand, hardly moves at all).

    c. Mendelssohn, Piano Trio (the right-hand melody is a memorable,
        beautiful tune; the left-hand melody is an accompaniment to it).

5-4. Use arrows to connect each note on the great staff to the corresponding key on the keyboard. Your arrows should extend all the way to the proper key and they may not cross.

Name: _____

Date: _____

Instructor's Name: _____

5-5. For each indicated key on the keyboard, write the corresponding note on the great staff.

Chapter 1: Supplementary Lesson

In this lesson you will learn about alto clef, tenor clef, octave signs (*8va* and *8vb*), octave designations, double flats, and double sharps.

Clefs are used to assign pitches to specific locations on the musical staff. In addition to the treble and bass clefs studied previously, there is a group of clefs known as **C clefs** because they assign middle C to different lines of the staff. Of the C clefs, the most important are **alto clef,** which assigns middle C to the third line of the staff, and **tenor clef,** which assigns middle C to the fourth line of the staff. The alto clef is used primarily by the viola. The tenor clef is used by cello, bassoon, and trombone when their notes get too high to be written comfortably in their more usual bass clef. Which clef is used depends on custom and ease of writing notes without recourse to cumbersome ledger lines. Alto and tenor clefs are written in the same way: two vertical lines and two loops surrounding the line that represents middle C.

C clefs
Alto clef
Tenor clef

alto clef: viola
• middle C = 3rd line
(a = comes 1st, 3 before 4)
tenor clef:
• middle C = 4th line
• cello, bassoon, trombone

Too low for treble clef (viola melody from Haydn, String Quartet)

Just right for alto clef (same melody)

Too high for bass clef (cello melody from Beethoven, Symphony No. 5)

Just right for tenor clef (same melody) *4th line (clef shows up higher)*

The highest and lowest notes require many ledger lines, and these can be confusing and hard to read. Instead, composers often use the **octave sign (8va)** to indicate that notes should be played an octave higher than written or *8vb* for notes that should be played an octave lower than written.

Octave sign

8va

8vb

Octave
sign

Octave designation

To identify a specific pitch, we will need to use not only its letter name but also its **octave designation.** Middle C, for example, is known as C4—it's the note C positioned at the beginning of the 4-octave. All of the notes above middle C, but lower than the next higher C, also lie in the 4-octave. (Octave designations actually depend on the letter name of the note, so B♯4 is in the 4-octave, although it is higher in pitch than C♭5). Every pitch can be precisely identified with a letter name and an octave designation. Our work in this book takes place between C2 and E6, as does most music.

Octave designations

C2 D2 E2 F2 G2 A2 B2 C3 D3 E3 F3 G3 A3 B3 C4 D4 E4 F4 G4 A4 B4 C5 D5 E5 F5 G5 A5 B5 C6 D6 E6

4-octave   5-octave   6-octave

3-octave

middle = C4

2-octave

Another more traditional system of octave designations is also in use.

Traditional octave designations

Traditional system	CC	C	c	c1	c2	c3	c4
	Contra	Great	Small	1-line	2-line	3-line	4-line

8va

8vb

**Double sharp
Double flat**

The most commonly used accidentals are the sharp sign (which raises a note by one semitone), the flat sign (which lowers a note by one semitone), and the natural sign (which cancels any previous sharp or flat). In addition, it is also possible to raise a note by two semitones using a **double sharp** sign or to lower a note by two semitones using a **double flat** sign.

A double sharp sign is made with a <u>simple small x</u> before the note. A double flat sign is made with <u>two flat signs</u> just touching each other.

Chapter 1: Self-Test

1. Identify these notes (treble clef):

B   F   E♭   C   G♯   A   C♯   B   B   E   A♭   F♯   G   C

2. Write these notes (treble clef):
(There will be more than one correct answer.)

B   D♯   G   C   B♭   A   E♭   F♯   D   A♭   G♯

3. Identify these notes (bass clef):

F   C♯   B   G   E   A♭   F♯   B♭   D   D   A   E   C

4. Write these notes (bass clef):
(There will be more than one correct answer.)

F♯   E♭   G   E   B♭   A♯   C♯   A   F   C

5. For each indicated key on the keyboard, write the corresponding note on the great staff.

6. For each note on the great staff, draw an arrow to the corresponding key on the keyboard.

Chapter 1: Self-Test (answer key)

1. Identify these notes (treble clef):

B   F   Eb   C   G#   A   C#   B   B   E   Ab   F#   G   C

2. Write these notes (treble clef):
   (Multiple correct answers are provided for each item.)

B   D#   G   C   Bb   A   Eb   F#   D   Ab   G#

3. Identify these notes (bass clef):

F   C#   B   G   E   Ab   F#   Bb   D   D   A   E   C

4. Write these notes (bass clef):
   (Multiple correct answers are provided for each item.)

F#   Eb   G   E   Bb   A#   C#   A   F   C

5. For each indicated key on the keyboard, write the corresponding note on the great staff.

6. For each note on the great staff, draw an arrow to the corresponding key on the keyboard.

2 Rhythm and Meter

Lesson 6: Quarter notes, half notes, and whole notes in ⁴⁄₄ meter

---

In this lesson you will learn about quarter notes, half notes, whole notes, stems, beats, measures (bars) and barlines, ⁴⁄₄ meter ("common time"), upbeat, downbeat, accent, conducting patterns, and tempo.

↱ melodic motion

Just as **pitch** measures musical activity in **space** (high and low, up and down), **rhythm** measures musical activity in **time** (longer and shorter, before and after). The most common unit of musical duration is called a **quarter note**, and it is written with a filled-in notehead and a **stem** (a vertical line that extends up or down from a notehead). Two quarter notes together make a **half note**, which is written as an open notehead with a stem. Similarly, two half notes combine to make a **whole note**, which is written as an open notehead with no stem.

note value = length of the note (that its played)

Rhythm - how fast notes move
Quarter note in time relative
Stem   to tempo
Half note

Whole note

Quarter notes — ¹⁄₄

Half notes — ¹⁄₂

Whole notes — whole

These three rhythmic values create a hierarchy of durations, from relatively short to relatively long, all in proportion to each other.

Use the staves that follow to practice writing quarter, half, and whole notes. The stem should be an octave in length. When the notehead is on the second space of the staff or lower, the stem goes up (from the right side of the notehead). When the notehead is on the third line of the staff or higher, the stem goes down (from the left side of the notehead).

✳ stems going:
- in right direction AND
- stems on right side of
the note: ♩ or ♀

3ʳᵈ line = goes down. Below that, goes up ↑!

Models   Write ten more

Whole notes

Half notes

Quarter notes

Beat
Measures
Bars
Barlines
Time signature

The quarter note usually serves as the **beat:** a steady, regular pulsation. The beats are grouped into **measures** (also called **bars**), which are separated by **barlines** (vertical lines through the staff). At the end of a piece or exercise, a double barline is used. A **time signature** is used to indicate which note value is acting as the beat and how many beats there are in the measure. It consists of two numbers written in a vertical stack. The number on the bottom tells which note value is acting as the beat: 4 for the quarter note, 2 for the half note, and (much less commonly) 1 for the whole note. (Other rhythmic values also can function as the beat, as we will see in later lessons.) The number on top tells how many beats there are per measure. The time signature $\frac{4}{4}$, for example, indicates that each measure contains four quarter notes. That arrangement of beats in the measure is the music's **meter.**

top # : how many of those in measure
bottom # : is the beat

Meter

$\frac{4}{4}$ meter

bar lines

2nd measure

$\frac{4}{4}$ Meter
Common time

$\frac{4}{4}$ **meter** is used so often that it is called **common time.** Sometimes, the symbol **c** is used instead of $\frac{4}{4}$.

Common time

Within a particular meter like $\frac{4}{4}$, the actual note values need not be quarter notes so long as each measure contains the durational equivalent of four quarter notes. A measure of $\frac{4}{4}$ might contain one whole note, or two half notes, or four quarter notes, or any combination of quarter and half notes that adds up to the equivalent of four quarter notes. The rhythms may vary, but the meter stays the same.

Rhythms in $\frac{4}{4}$

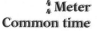

Downbeat
Accent

Upbeat

Each beat in $\frac{4}{4}$ meter has a distinctive character. The first beat of the measure is called the **downbeat**, and it receives a particular weight or **accent**. It sounds relatively strong and heavy compared to the other beats of the measure—rhythmic movement seems to depart from and return to it. The fourth beat of the measure is called the **upbeat** and, although it is relatively weak, it gives a strong sense of directed, dynamic motion toward the downbeat. The third beat receives a secondary accent—weaker than the actual downbeat, but stronger than the weak second beat that leads to it.

Accentuation in $\frac{4}{4}$

Conducting pattern

This pattern of accentuation is reflected in the gestures that a conductor uses to convey a feeling of $\frac{4}{4}$. Use your right hand and follow this **conducting pattern:** down for beat 1 (the downbeat); left for beat 2; right for beat 3; then back up for beat 4 (the upbeat).

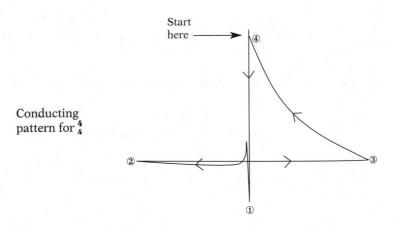

Conducting pattern for $\frac{4}{4}$

The speed of the beats—how rapidly they occur—is called the **tempo.** Tempo can be indicated in two ways: with a one-word character description (customarily in Italian) or with the number of beats per minute. Here are some common tempo names and associated numbers of beats per minute (these are approximate).

Tempo	Names	Adagio Slowly	Andante Somewhat slowly	Moderato Moderately	Allegro Fast	Presto Very fast
	Beats per minute	50	72	96	120	152

Lesson 6: In-class activities

1. **Dictation.** Within each group, the instructor will perform the three rhythms in a random order. Identify the rhythm you hear and tap it back. (The activities in this and subsequent lessons in this chapter make use of the single-line staff commonly used for percussion instruments. The usual five-line staff, used to indicate pitch, is not needed.)

2. Solo. Suggestions for performance: (1) another member of the class claps the beats (or just the downbeat of each measure) while you clap or tap the given rhythm; (2) stamp your foot on each downbeat while clapping the rhythm, or tapping it, or chanting it using the syllable "ta"; (3) tap the four beats of the measure with your hand while chanting the rhythm using the syllable "ta"; (4) say the beats of the measure (1-2-3-4) while tapping the rhythm with your hand; (5) tap the beats with one hand while tapping the rhythm with the other; (6) conduct the beats with your right hand while chanting the rhythm using the syllable "ta." It is a good idea to tap four preparatory beats, or count 1-2-3-4, or conduct one preparatory measure before beginning each exercise in order to establish the tempo.

3. Duets. Suggestions for performance: (1) one student or group of students performs each part of the duet, either tapping or chanting "ta." Then switch parts; (2) a single student chants the higher rhythm while tapping the lower and then vice versa.

4. Improvisation. You are given two measures of a rhythm in $\frac{4}{4}$. Using only whole notes, half notes, and quarter notes, continue and conclude by improvising two more measures. In your improvisation, use the rhythmic values and ideas found in the two measures you are given. Perform your improvisation by clapping your hands, tapping on your desk, or chanting using the syllable "ta." Three suggestions for performance: (1) improvise a two-measure continuation and conclusion; (2) perform your improvisation in continuing succession with other students, in tempo and without missing a beat. As one student concludes an improvisation, another begins immediately, by performing all four measures (beginning with the two given measures) or just the two-measure improvisation; (3) after you complete an improvisation, another student may be asked to perform what he or she heard you do. The example that follows shows three possible continuations for a given opening.

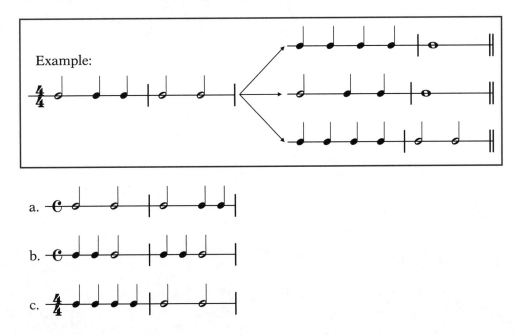

Name: _____

Date: _____

Instructor's Name: _____

LESSON 6: EXERCISES

6-1. Insert barlines to create complete measures in $\frac{4}{4}$ meter. (The exercises in this and subsequent lessons in this chapter make use of the single-line staff commonly used for percussion instruments. The usual five-line staff, used to indicate pitch, is not needed.)

6-2. There are blank places, indicated with an arrow, in some of these measures in $\frac{4}{4}$ meter. Fill them in by adding one or more notes of the proper time-value. Remember to use quarter notes, half notes, and whole notes only.

mysearchlab

6-3. Continue and complete the following short rhythmic compositions. Each will be six measures long. Be prepared to perform your compositions in class. Remember to use quarter notes, half notes, and whole notes only.

6-4. Set the following poetic texts to an appropriate rhythm. Each syllable should receive one note. Accented syllables should be placed in accented parts of the measure; unaccented syllables should be placed in unaccented parts of the measure. You should write complete, correct measures in $\frac{4}{4}$ using only quarter, half, and whole notes. Each setting is begun for you. Use as many measures as you feel you need. Be prepared to perform your settings in class.

Example:
To provide a rhythmic setting for the following text, begin by reading it aloud and determine which of its syllables is accented (marked with /) and which is unaccented (marked with ‿):

/ ‿ / ‿ / ‿ /   ‿ / ‿‿ / ‿
What a piece of work is man! How noble in reason!

Then provide a rhythmic setting that locates the accented syllables on the strong beats of the measure (beats 1 and 3) and the unaccented syllables on the weak beats of the measure (beats 2 and 4). Be sure to provide a note for each syllable of the text and to write complete, correct measures. Here is one reasonable setting; there are certainly others (your own taste and artistic sense will guide you).

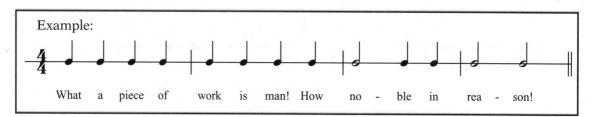

Name: _____

Date: _____

Instructor's Name: _____

a. Do not go gentle into that good night.
   Rage, rage against the dying of the light.
   (Dylan Thomas)

Do   not   go   gen - tle

b. When in disgrace with fortune and men's eyes,
   I all alone beweep my outcast state.
   (William Shakespeare)

When   in   dis   -   grace

6-5. Set your own full name to an appropriate rhythm. Each syllable should receive a note. Accented syllables should be placed on accented beats of the measure; unaccented syllables should be placed on unaccented beats of the measure. You should write complete, correct measures in $\frac{4}{4}$ using only quarter, half, and whole notes. Be prepared to perform your setting in class.

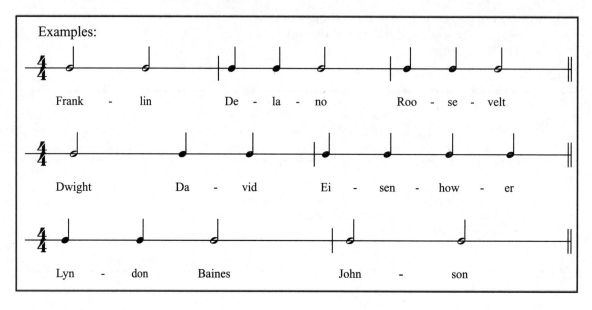

Examples:

Frank - lin   De - la - no   Roo - se - velt

Dwight   Da - vid   Ei - sen - how - er

Lyn - don   Baines   John - son

Your name here:

Lesson 7: Eighth notes and sixteenth notes

In this lesson you will learn about eighth notes and sixteenth notes, flags, and beams.

Just as quarter notes can be combined to create longer durations, they can be divided to create shorter ones. A quarter note can be divided into two **eighth notes**. Eighth notes are written with a filled-in notehead and a stem with a **flag**. When two eighth notes occur together in a pair, it is customary to dispense with the flags and join them with a **beam**, a horizontal line that connects the stems. Four eighth notes together also can be joined with a beam.

Eighth notes
Flag — *goes to the right*

Beam

Quarter notes

Eighth notes
with flags

Eighth notes
with beams

Use the staves that follow to practice writing eighth notes. The flag attaches at the top of an upward stem and at the bottom of a downward stem, then curves out to the right and back toward the notehead. Notice that although the stem switches sides of the notehead depending on its direction (upward stems attach to the right side of the notehead and downward stems to the left side), flags **always** go to the right side of the stem. The beam is a horizontal line that connects the ends of the stems.

Eighth notes
with flags

Models   Write sixteen more

Eighth notes
with beams

An eighth note can be divided into two **sixteenth notes**. A sixteenth note is written with a filled-in notehead and a stem with a **double flag**. Like eighth notes, sixteenth notes that occur in pairs or groups of four can be written with beams instead of flags. It is also possible for eighth notes and sixteenth notes to share a beam.

Sixteenth notes
Double flag

Eighth notes

Sixteenth notes

Double beam   Use the staves that follow to practice writing sixteenth notes with double
flags and **double beams.**

Use beams to clarify the beats, not to obscure them. Beams should not
span across the boundary between the beats, particularly between beats 2 and 3,
and they may not begin in the middle of a beat. It is common, however, for
four eighth notes to share a beam for beats 1 and 2 or beats 3 and 4.

In deciding if the stems will go up to a beam above the staff or down to a
beam below it, the note farthest from the center line is the deciding factor: If
the most distant note is higher than the center line, the stems go down, and if
it is lower than the center line, the stems go up.

If there is a tie under this distance rule, then majority rules: If most of
the stems would go up (because the notes lie below the middle line), then all
the stems go up to the beam; if most of the stems would go down (because the
notes lie higher than the middle line), then all the stems go down to the beam.

Sometimes in writing for singers, composers don't use beams at all. Instead,
if a syllable of text receives an eighth note or sixteenth note, it will have its own
flag. In the written exercises for this book, however, we will normally use beams.

So now we have five different rhythmic values, or time-values: sixteenth, eighth, quarter, half, and whole notes. These range from the relatively short to the relatively long, all in arithmetical proportion to each other.

Proportional rhythms

Lesson 7: In-class activities

1. Dictation. Within each group, the instructor will perform the three rhythms in a random order. Identify the rhythm you hear and tap it back.

2. Solo. Suggestions for performance: (1) another member of the class claps the beats (or just the downbeat of each measure) while you clap or tap the given rhythm; (2) stamp your foot on each downbeat while clapping the rhythm, or tapping it, or chanting it using the syllable "ta"; (3) tap the four beats of the measure with your hand while chanting the rhythm using the syllable "ta"; (4) say the beats of the measure (1-2-3-4) while tapping the rhythm with your hand; (5) tap the beats with one hand while tapping the rhythm with the other; (6) conduct the beats with your right hand while chanting the rhythm using the syllable "ta." It is a good idea to tap four preparatory beats, or count 1-2-3-4, or conduct one preparatory measure before beginning each exercise in order to establish the tempo.

a. **Andante**

b. **Adagio**

c. ♩ = 72

d. Arlen, "Over the Rainbow" (adapted)

   Moderately

e. Mozart, Sonata (adapted)

   Allegro

f. Bach, Fugue in G minor

3. **Duets.** Suggestions for performance: (1) one student or group of students performs each part of the duet, either tapping or chanting "ta." Then switch parts; (2) a single student chants the higher rhythm while tapping the lower and then vice versa.

4. Improvisation. You are given two measures of a rhythm in $\frac{4}{4}$. With whole notes, half notes, quarter notes, eighth notes, and sixteenth notes available to you, continue and conclude by improvising two more measures. In your improvisation, use the rhythmic values and ideas found in the two measures you are given. Perform your improvisation by clapping your hands, tapping on your desk, or chanting using the syllable "ta." Three suggestions for performance: (1) improvise a two-measure continuation and conclusion; (2) perform your improvisation in continuing succession with other students, in tempo and without missing a beat. As one student concludes an improvisation, another begins immediately, by performing all four measures (beginning with the two given measures) or just the two-measure improvisation; (3) after you complete an improvisation, another student may be asked to perform what he or she heard you do. The example that follows shows three possible continuations for a given opening.

Name: _____

Date: _____

Instructor's Name: _____

*Test 2: writing
beams + correcting
stem directions
— choose note that's farther
away from midline*

LESSON 7: EXERCISES

7-1. Insert barlines to create complete measures in $\frac{4}{4}$ meter.

7-2. There are blank places, indicated with arrows, in some of these measures in $\frac{4}{4}$ meter. Fill them in by adding one or more notes of the proper time-value. Remember to use use <u>whole</u>, <u>half</u>, <u>quarter</u>, <u>eighth</u>, and <u>sixteenth</u> notes only.

PEARSON
mysearchlab

7-3. Rewrite the following rhythms using beams instead of flags.

7-4. Continue and complete the following short rhythmic compositions. Each is four measures in length. Be prepared to perform your compositions in class. Remember to use whole, half, quarter, eighth, and sixteenth notes only.

Name: _____

Date: _____

Instructor's Name: _____

7-5. Set the following poetic texts to an appropriate rhythm. Each syllable should receive a note. Accented syllables should be placed in accented parts of the measure; unaccented syllables should be placed in unaccented parts of the measure. You should write complete, correct measures in $\frac{4}{4}$ using whole notes, half notes, quarter notes, eighth notes, and sixteenth notes as appropriate. Each setting is begun for you. Use as many measures as you feel you need. Be prepared to perform your settings in class. (See Exercise 6-4 for an example of the proper procedure.)

Note: In vocal music, composers traditionally use a separate stem and flag for each syllable of text, without beams; this practice can be seen throughout the anthology at the end of this book. In the written exercises, however, students are asked (at the discretion of the instructor) to use beams in the manner of instrumental music.

a. Whither is fled the visionary gleam?
   Where is it now, the glory and the dream?
   (William Wordsworth)

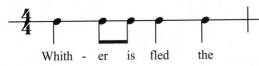

b. Let us go then, you and I,
   When the evening is spread out against the sky
   Like a patient etherized upon a table.
   (T. S. Eliot)

Lesson 8: Dots and ties

In this lesson you will learn about the augmentation dot, dotted rhythms, ties, and anacrusis.

An **augmentation dot** placed directly after a note increases the time-value of that note by one half. In principle, any note can have its value increased in this way, but as a practical matter, we will be talking about three dotted notes: dotted half notes, dotted quarter notes, and dotted eighth notes. (When the notehead is on the line of the staff, the augmentation dot is placed just above the line.)

Augmentation dot

Augmentation dot

The augmentation dot gives us three new rhythmic figures called **dotted rhythms** by combining a dotted half with a quarter, a dotted quarter with an eighth, and a dotted eighth with a sixteenth. In each case, a larger value is divided into two unequal parts.

Dotted rhythms

Dotted rhythms

Notice that a dotted eighth note and a sixteenth note that combine into a quarter note beat can be beamed together.

Dotted eighth and sixteenth

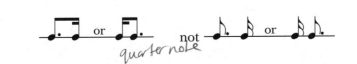

quarter note

Tie
[handwritten: samenote (pitch)]

Still more rhythmic values become available through the use of the **tie**. A tie is a curved line that connects two notes of the **same** pitch. It combines those two notes into a single note whose duration is the sum of the two notes. Notice that ties always join noteheads, never stems.

[handwritten: • to join note into next measure OR beat grouping]

Ties

[handwritten: ✱ making note longer (join note values tog)]

Slur
[handwritten: • connecting diff. notes.]

A **slur**, in contrast, is an articulation mark used to suggest a smooth connection between two or more **different** notes. Slurs and ties are both created with curved lines, but the slur does not affect the rhythmic values.

Do not allow a dotted note to obscure the beats of the measure, particularly beat 3. Ties should be used instead.

Correct   Incorrect

Ties vs. Dots

[handwritten: obscures 3rd beat.]

[handwritten: obscuring 3rd beat.]

Anacrusis

A piece of music may begin on the downbeat (first beat) of a measure or it may begin in the middle of an incomplete measure. An incomplete preliminary measure is called an **anacrusis**, **upbeat**, or **pickup**. By convention, when a piece begins with an anacrusis it will end with an incomplete measure. The durations of the anacrusis and the final measure combined will be equal to one full measure. For example, in $\frac{4}{4}$, if the anacrusis is one beat long, the final measure will be three beats long.

Anacrusis

anacrusis
(1 beat)

incomplete
final measure
(3 beats)

Lesson 8: In-class activities

1. **Dictation.** Within each group, the instructor will perform the three rhythms in a random order. Identify the rhythm you hear and tap it back.

2. **Solo.** Suggestions for performance: (1) another member of the class claps the beats (or just the downbeat of each measure) while you clap or tap the given rhythm; (2) stamp your foot on each downbeat while clapping the rhythm, or tapping it, or chanting it using the syllable "ta"; (3) tap the four beats of the measure with your hand while chanting the rhythm using the syllable "ta"; (4) say the beats of the measure (1-2-3-4) while tapping the rhythm with your hand; (5) tap the beats with one hand while tapping the rhythm with the other; (6) conduct the beats with your right hand while chanting the rhythm using the syllable "ta." It is a good idea to tap four preparatory beats, or count 1-2-3-4, or conduct one preparatory measure before beginning each exercise in order to establish the tempo.

a. Bach, Chorale

b. Mozart, "Dove sono"

c. Mendelssohn, Piano Trio (half of the measures in this passage have the same rhythmic pattern: a dotted quarter note followed by five eighth notes).

d. Chopin, Prelude in C minor (all four measures share the same rhythmic pattern).

3. Duets. Suggestions for performance: (1) one student or group of students performs each part of the duet, either tapping or chanting "ta." Then switch parts; (2) a single student chants the upper rhythm while tapping the lower and then vice versa.

4. Improvisation. You are given two measures of a rhythm in $\frac{4}{4}$. With whole notes, half notes, quarter notes, eighth notes, and sixteenth notes available to you, as well as dotted rhythms, continue and conclude by improvising two more measures. In your improvisation, use the rhythmic values and ideas found in the two measures you are given. Perform your improvisation by clapping your hands, tapping on your desk, or chanting using the syllable "ta." Three suggestions for performance: (1) improvise a two-measure continuation and conclusion; (2) perform your improvisation in continuing succession with other students, in tempo and without missing a beat. As one student concludes an improvisation, another begins immediately, either by performing all four measures (beginning with the two given measures) or just the two-measure improvisation; (3) after you complete an improvisation, another student may be asked to perform what he or she heard you do. The example that follows shows three possible continuations for a given opening.

Name: _____

Date: _____

Instructor's Name: _____

LESSON 8: EXERCISES

8-1. Insert barlines to create complete measures in $\frac{4}{4}$ meter.

8-2. There are blank places, indicated with arrows, in some of these measures in $\frac{4}{4}$ meter. Fill them in by adding one or more notes of the proper time-value. Use at least one dotted rhythm in each exercise.

don't obscure

mysearchlab

8-3. Rewrite these rhythms using dots instead of ties.

8-4. Continue and complete the following short rhythmic compositions. Each should be four measures in length. Be sure to use dotted rhythms and ties. Be prepared to perform your compositions in class.

Name: _____

Date: _____

Instructor's Name: _____

8-5. Set the following poetic texts to an appropriate rhythm. Each syllable should receive a note. Accented syllables should be placed in accented parts of the measure; unaccented syllables should be placed in unaccented parts of the measure. You should write complete, correct measures in $\frac{4}{4}$ using whole notes, half notes, quarter notes, eighth notes, sixteenth notes, and dotted rhythms as appropriate. Each setting is begun for you. Use as many measures as you feel you need. Be prepared to perform your settings in class. (See Exercise 6-4 for an example of the proper procedure.)

mysearchlab

Note: In vocal music, composers traditionally use a separate stem and flag for each syllable of text, without beams; this practice can be seen throughout the anthology. In the written exercises, however, students are asked (at the discretion of the instructor) to use beams in the manner of instrumental music.

a. O body swayed to music, O brightening glance,
   How can we know the dancer from the dance?
   (W. B. Yeats)

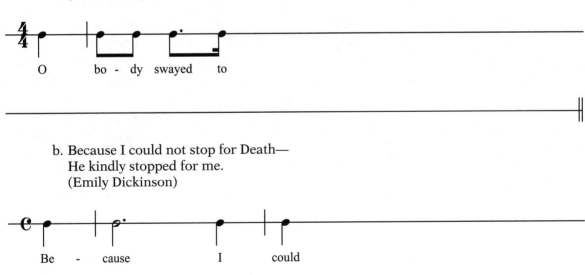

O   bo - dy swayed to

b. Because I could not stop for Death—
   He kindly stopped for me.
   (Emily Dickinson)

Be - cause   I   could

Lesson 9: Rests

In this lesson you will learn about rests.

Any rhythmic value can be represented by either a note or a **rest**. A rest is a
silence of a certain duration. First let's consider rests that last for the duration
of a whole note, half note, or quarter note.

Rest

Rests *[handwritten: hangs down from 4th line] [handwritten: from 3rd line!! →up]*

The whole-note and half-note rests are written using the same shape, but
the whole-note rest hangs below the fourth line of the staff and the half-note
rest sits on the middle line. The squiggly quarter-note rest lies between the
lowest and highest spaces of the staff. Use the staves that follow to practice
writing whole-note, half-note, and quarter-note rests.

[handwritten right margin: ← group of 4 grouping]
[handwritten: = 4 notes]
[handwritten: = 2 notes]

[handwritten: If: ♪ 𝄾 𝄾𝄾]

Write whole-note rests.

Write half-note rests.

Write quarter-note rests.

Note that in $\frac{4}{4}$ meter, two quarter-note rests on beats 1-2 and 3-4 are normally combined into a single half-note rest. Half-note rests, however, are not
used to span beats 2-3.

Correct   Incorrect *[handwritten: reduce to half note rest]*

**Using half-note and
quarter-note rests**

[handwritten: - HAS to be on beats 1 or 3 (can't be on beat 2 !!)]

[handwritten: (is obscuring 3rd -]

[handwritten: grouping beats & rests. - grouping is by the half measure.]

The eighth-note rest is a diagonal straight line with a short flag attached at
the top. The sixteenth-note rest is formed the same way, but with a double flag.

Eighth-note rests

[handwritten: can't obscure 3rd beat]

Sixteenth-note rests

[handwritten: If have a short group. Must nosh off the 1st half of it — my group of 4 notes]
[handwritten: ♪ 𝄾 𝄾 | ♪ 𝄾 | ♪ 𝄾 𝄾 | · don't obscure the 3rd note!!]
[handwritten: X   X   ✓]

Use the staves that follow to practice writing eighth-note and sixteenth-note rests.

Write eighth-note rests.

Write sixteenth-note rests.

As with notes, adding a dot to a rest increases its length by half.

Dotted rests

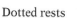

In practice, the dotted half-note rest is not used in $\frac{4}{4}$ meter, because a half-note rest and a separate quarter-note rest better respect the accent on the third beat of the measure.

Dotted half-note
rest in $\frac{4}{4}$

Correct   Incorrect

obscuring!

Note that while rests may be dotted, they may not be tied.

Lesson 9: In-class activities

1. Dictation. Within each group, the instructor will perform the three rhythms in a random order. Identify the rhythm you hear and tap it back.

2. Solo. Suggestions for performance: (1) another member of the class claps the beats (or just the downbeat of each measure) while you clap or tap the given rhythm; (2) stamp your foot on each downbeat while clapping the rhythm, or tapping it, or chanting it using the syllable "ta"; (3) tap the four beats of the measure with your hand while chanting the rhythm using the syllable "ta"; (4) say the beats of the measure (1-2-3-4) while tapping the rhythm with your hand; (5) tap the beats with one hand while tapping the rhythm with the other; (6) conduct the beats with your right hand while chanting the rhythm using the syllable "ta." It is a good idea to tap four preparatory beats, or count 1-2-3-4, or conduct one preparatory measure before beginning each exercise in order to establish the tempo.

e. Bach, Fugue in G minor (both measures start with a rest and end with two quarter notes).

f. Mozart, "Dove sono" (this phrase begins with an anacrusis, a pickup to the first measure).

g. Mozart, Sonata (the rests in measure 3 occur on the beat, while the eighth notes occur after the beat—that's a *syncopation*, a topic to be discussed in Lesson 13).

3. Duets. Suggestions for performance: (1) one student or group of students performs each part of the duet, either tapping or chanting "ta." Then switch parts; (2) a single student chants the higher rhythm while tapping the lower and then vice versa.

d.

4. Improvisation. You are given two measures of a rhythm in $\frac{4}{4}$. With whole notes, half notes, quarter notes, eighth notes, and sixteenth notes available to you, as well as dotted rhythms and rests, continue and conclude by improvising two more measures. In your improvisation, use the rhythmic values and ideas found in the two measures you are given. Perform your improvisation by clapping your hands, tapping on your desk, or chanting using the syllable "ta." Three suggestions for performance: (1) improvise a two-measure continuation and conclusion; (2) perform your improvisation in continuing succession with other students, in tempo and without missing a beat. As one student concludes an improvisation, another begins immediately, either by performing all four measures (beginning with the two given measures) or just the two-measure improvisation; (3) after you complete an improvisation, another student may be asked to perform what he or she heard you do. The example that follows shows three possible continuations for a given opening.

Name: _____

Date: _____

Instructor's Name: _____

LESSON 9: EXERCISES

9-1. Rewrite the rhythms that follow, replacing each note with a rest of the
same time-value.

a.

*⊁ middle of bar
for whole rests!!!*

b.

9-2. Insert barlines to create complete measures in $\frac{4}{4}$ meter.

a.

b.

c.

mysearchlab   9-3. There are blank spots, indicated with arrows, in some of these measures in $\frac{4}{4}$ meter. Fill in with a single rest to create complete measures of $\frac{4}{4}$.

MORE

mysearchlab   9-4. Continue and complete the following short rhythmic compositions. Each should be four measures in length. Be sure to use rests. Be prepared to perform your compositions in class.

Name: _____

Date: _____

Instructor's Name: _____

9-5. Set the following poetic texts to an appropriate rhythm. Each syllable should receive a note. Accented syllables should be placed in accented parts of the measure; unaccented syllables should be placed in unaccented parts of the measure. You should write complete, correct measures in $\frac{4}{4}$ using whole notes, half notes, quarter notes, eighth notes, sixteenth notes, dotted rhythms, and rests as appropriate. Each setting is begun for you. Use as many measures as you feel you need. Be prepared to perform your settings in class. (See Exercise 6-4 for an example of the proper procedure.)

Note: In vocal music, composers traditionally use a separate stem and flag for each syllable of text, without beams; this practice can be seen throughout the anthology at the end of this book. In the written exercises, however, students are asked (at the discretion of the instructor) to use beams in the manner of instrumental music.

a. O Captain! my Captain! our fearful trip is done.
   (Walt Whitman)

b. Heard melodies are sweet, but those unheard
   Are sweeter; therefore, ye soft pipes, play on.
   (John Keats)

Lesson 10: Duple meter (²⁄₄ and ²⁄₂)   *grouped by ♩ note*

In this lesson you will learn about ²⁄₄ and ²⁄₂ meter, **alla breve** ¢, upbeat, downbeat, and conducting patterns.   *↑ = ²⁄₂*

↳ common time w / line thru ¢ → man...

In ²⁄₄ **meter,** each measure consists of the time-value of two quarter notes.

²⁄₄ Meter

²⁄₄ meter

As with ⁴⁄₄, discussed in the previous lessons, the actual note values need not be quarter notes so long as each measure contains the durational equivalent of two quarter notes. A measure of ²⁄₄ might contain one half note, two quarter notes, four eighth notes, eight sixteenth notes, or any combination of those rhythmic values that adds up to a total duration equivalent to two quarter notes.

²⁄₄ meter

As with ⁴⁄₄, the beats of ²⁄₄ meter have a different character. The first beat of the measure is the **downbeat**. It is relatively strong and receives an **accent**; it gives a sense of stability and arrival. The second beat of the measure is the **upbeat**. It is relatively weak and unaccented; it gives a sense of dynamic motion that leads to the downbeat.

Downbeat
Accent
Upbeat

Downbeat and upbeat

²⁄₄ is a **duple meter** because its measure contains two beats. Another important duple meter is ²⁄₂, a measure that contains two half-note beats. A measure of ²⁄₂ has the same duration as a measure of ⁴⁄₄, but has only two half-note beats instead of four quarter-note beats. The time signature for ²⁄₂ is often written with the symbol ¢. This meter is sometimes called **alla breve,** which is another way of saying that the measure contains two half-note beats (breves).

Duple meter
²⁄₂ Meter

Alla breve

↳ mainly half note groupings
· usually faster tempo compared to ⁴⁄₄

²⁄₂ meter

As with ⁴⁄₄ and ²⁄₄, a variety of rhythmic patterns can be used in ²⁄₂. The pattern of accents is the same in ²⁄₂ as in ²⁄₄: the measure consists of a weighted downbeat and a relatively weak upbeat.

²⁄₂ meter

Conducting
pattern

The **conducting pattern** is the same for both meters and reflects this pattern of accents.

Conducting
pattern for
$\frac{2}{4}$ and $\frac{2}{2}$

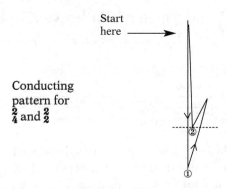

Lesson 10: In-class activities

1. **Dictation.** Within each group, the instructor will perform the three rhythms in a random order. Identify the rhythm you hear and tap it back.

2. **Solo.** Suggestions for performance: (1) another member of the class claps the beats (or just the downbeat of each measure) while you clap or tap the given rhythm; (2) stamp your foot on each downbeat while clapping the rhythm, or tapping it, or chanting it using the syllable "ta"; (3) tap the two beats of the measure with your hand while chanting the rhythm using the syllable "ta"; (4) say the beats of the measure (1-2) while tapping the rhythm with your hand; (5) tap the beats with one hand while tapping the rhythm with the other; (6) conduct the beats with your right hand while chanting the rhythm using the syllable "ta." It is a good idea to tap two preparatory beats, or count 1-2, or conduct one preparatory measure before beginning each exercise in order to establish the tempo.

a. Mozart, "Dove sono" (the rhythm in measures 1–4 is the same as in measures 9–12).

b. Schubert, "Heidenröslein" (this music uses flags instead of beams for eighth notes. That is common in vocal music, where each syllable of the text receives a note, and the notes have their own flags).

c. Arlen, "Over the Rainbow" (the rhythm in measures 1–2 is the same as in measures 5–6).

d. Rodríguez, "La Cumparsita" (the rhythm in measures 1–2 is the same as in measures 3–4).

3. Duets. Suggestions for performance: (1) one student or group of students performs each part of the duet, either tapping or chanting "ta." Then switch parts; (2) a single student chants the higher rhythm while tapping the lower and then vice versa.

4. Improvisation. You are given four measures of a rhythm in either $\frac{2}{4}$ or $\frac{2}{2}$. With whole notes, half notes, quarter notes, eighth notes, and sixteenth notes available to you, as well as dotted rhythms and rests, continue and conclude by improvising four more measures. In your improvisation, use the rhythmic values and ideas found in the four measures you are given. Perform your improvisation by clapping your hands, tapping on your desk, or chanting using the syllable "ta." Three suggestions for performance: (1) improvise a four-measure continuation and conclusion; (2) perform your improvisation in continuing succession with other students, in tempo and without missing a beat. As one student concludes an improvisation, another begins immediately, either by performing all eight measures (beginning with the four given measures) or just the four-measure improvisation; (3) after you complete an improvisation, another student may be asked to perform what he or she heard you do. The example that follows shows three possible continuations for a given opening.

Name: _____

Date: _____

Instructor's Name: _____

LESSON 10: EXERCISES

10-1. Insert barlines to create complete measures in $\frac{2}{4}$ or $\frac{2}{2}$ meter.

10-2. There are blank places, indicated with arrows, in some of these measures in $\frac{2}{4}$ or $\frac{2}{2}$ meter. Fill them in by adding one or more notes of the proper time-value.

mysearchlab 10-3. Continue and complete the following short rhythmic compositions. Each should be six measures in length. Be prepared to perform your compositions in class.

mysearchlab 10-4. Set the following poetic texts to an appropriate rhythm. Each syllable should receive a note. Accented syllables should be placed in accented parts of the measure; unaccented syllables should be placed in unaccented parts of the measure. You should write complete, correct measures in $\frac{2}{4}$ or $\frac{2}{2}$ using whole notes, half notes, quarter notes, eighth notes, sixteenth notes, dotted rhythms, and rests as appropriate. Each setting is begun for you. Use as many measures as you feel you need. Be prepared to perform your settings in class. (See Exercise 6-4 for an example of the proper procedure.)

Note: In vocal music, composers traditionally use a separate stem and flag for each syllable of text, without beams; this practice can be seen throughout the anthology. In the written exercises, however, students are asked (at the discretion of the instructor) to use beams in the manner of instrumental music.

a. Made weak by time and fate, but strong in will
   To strive, to seek, to find, and not to yield.
   (Tennyson)

Name: _____

Date: _____

Instructor's Name: _____

    b. Since then, at an uncertain hour,
       That agony returns:
       And till my ghastly tale is told,
       This heart within me burns.
       (Coleridge)

Since   then,   at   an

Lesson 11: Triple meter ($\frac{3}{4}$)

In this lesson you will learn about $\frac{3}{4}$ meter and its conducting pattern.

$\frac{4}{4}$ is a **quadruple meter** because it divides the measure into four beats. $\frac{2}{4}$ and $\frac{2}{2}$ are **duple meters** because they divide the measure into two beats. The remaining principal kind of meter is **triple meter**, which divides the measure into three beats. $\frac{3}{8}$, $\frac{3}{4}$, and $\frac{3}{2}$ are all examples of triple meter and, of these, $\frac{3}{4}$ is the most commonly used.

Triple meter

$\frac{3}{4}$ **meter** indicates a measure that consists of three quarter-note beats.

$\frac{3}{4}$ **meter**

$\frac{3}{4}$ meter

A variety of rhythmic figures can be used in $\frac{3}{4}$ meter. Only the whole note $\times$ cannot be used—it is too long for the measure.

$\frac{3}{4}$ meter

When using rests in $\frac{3}{4}$, remember two rules: (1) a whole-note rest is used to fill the measure, not a dotted half-note rest; (2) a rest that lasts for two quarter notes should be indicated with two quarter-note rests, not one half-note rest.

Rests in $\frac{3}{4}$

4 note rest, not 3!!
Never 2 note rests in $\frac{3}{4}$

Cannot do any group of 2 rests!

As with the other meters we have discussed, the beats of $\frac{3}{4}$ have a distinctive character. The first beat is the downbeat and is strong compared to the other two. The third beat is an upbeat that leads to the downbeat. The second beat is a kind of echo or rebound from the first beat.

down, up, up

Accentuation in $\frac{3}{4}$

Conducting pattern

The **conducting pattern** for $\frac{3}{4}$ reflects the accentual pattern.

Conducting pattern for $\frac{3}{4}$

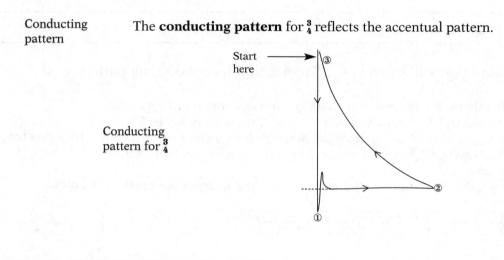

Lesson 11: In-class activities

1. **Dictation.** Within each group, the instructor will perform the three rhythms in a random order. identify the rhythm you hear and tap it back.

2. **Solo.** Suggestions for performance: (1) another member of the class claps the beats (or just the downbeat of each measure) while you clap or tap the given rhythm; (2) stamp your foot on each downbeat while clapping the rhythm, or tapping it, or chanting it using the syllable "ta"; (3) tap the three beats of the measure with your hand while chanting the rhythm using the syllable "ta"; (4) say the beats of the measure (1-2-3) while tapping the rhythm with your hand; (5) tap the beats with one hand while tapping the rhythm with the other; (6) conduct the beats with your right hand while chanting the rhythm using the syllable "ta." It is a good idea to tap three preparatory beats, or count 1-2-3, or conduct one preparatory measure before beginning each exercise in order to establish the tempo.

a. Schumann, Song (this passage makes frequent use of the rhythmic figure of a dotted eighth note and a sixteenth note).

b. Lang, Song (as in the Schumann song, the combination of a dotted eighth note and a sixteenth note is common in this passage).

c. Haydn, String Quartet (the rhythm in measures 56–58 is the same as in measures 60–62).

3. Duets. Suggestions for performance: (1) one student or group of students performs each part of the duet, either tapping or chanting "ta." Then switch parts; (2) a single student chants the higher rhythm while tapping the lower and then vice versa.

c. Chopin, Prelude (the upper part is just a bit more active rhythmically than the lower).

d. Haydn, String Quartet (these are the first violin and cello parts).

4. Improvisation. You are given four measures of a rhythm in $\frac{3}{4}$. With half notes, quarter notes, eighth notes, and sixteenth notes available to you, as well as dotted rhythms and rests, continue and conclude by improvising four more measures. In your improvisation, use the rhythmic values and ideas found in the four measures you are given. Perform your improvisation by clapping your hands, tapping on your desk, or chanting using the syllable "ta." Three suggestions for performance: (1) improvise a four-measure continuation and conclusion; (2) perform your improvisation in continuing succession with other students, in tempo and without missing a beat. As one student concludes an improvisation, another begins immediately, by performing all eight measures (beginning with the four given measures) or just the four-measure improvisation; (3) after you complete an improvisation, another student may be asked to perform what he or she heard you do. The example that follows shows three possible continuations for a given opening.

Example:

a.

b.

c.

Name: _____

Date: _____

Instructor's Name: _____

Lesson 11: Exercises

11-1. Insert barlines to create complete measures in $\frac{3}{4}$ meter.

11-2. There are blank places, indicated with arrows, in some of these measures in $\frac{3}{4}$ meter. Fill them in by adding one or more notes of the proper time-value.

11-3. Continue and complete the following short rhythmic compositions. Each should be four measures in length. Be prepared to perform your compositions in class.

b.

c.

d.

11-4. Set the following poetic texts to an appropriate rhythm. Each syllable should receive a note. Accented syllables should be placed in accented parts of the measure; unaccented syllables should be placed in unaccented parts of the measure. You should write complete, correct measures in $\frac{3}{4}$ using half notes, quarter notes, eighth notes, sixteenth notes, dotted rhythms, and rests as appropriate. Each setting is begun for you. Use as many measures as you feel you need. Be prepared to perform your settings in class. (See Exercise 6-4 for an example of the proper procedure.)

Note: In vocal music, composers traditionally use a separate stem and flag for each syllable of text, without beams; this practice can be seen throughout the anthology. In the written exercises, however, students are asked (at the discretion of the instructor) to use beams in the manner of instrumental music.

a. What passing-bells for these who die as cattle?
   Only the monstrous anger of the guns.
   (Wilfred Owen)

What   pass -   ing -   bells

b. And what rough beast, its hour come round at last,
   Slouches toward Bethlehem to be born?
   (W. B. Yeats)

And   what   rough beast,

Lesson 12: Compound meter ($\frac{6}{8}$)

In this lesson you will learn about compound meter, $\frac{6}{8}$ meter, and its conducting pattern.

The meters we have discussed so far ($\frac{4}{4}$, $\frac{2}{4}$, $\frac{2}{2}$, and $\frac{3}{4}$) are considered **simple meters** because their beats (quarter note or half note) are divided into **two** parts (eighth notes or quarter notes) and the beat itself is a simple value. In **compound meters,** in contrast, the beat is divided into **three** parts and the beat itself is a dotted note: a dotted eighth note, dotted quarter note, or dotted half note. In $\frac{6}{8}$ **meter,** for example, there are two dotted quarter-note beats per measure, and each beat is divided into three eighth notes.

Simple meter

Compound meter

$\frac{6}{8}$ **meter**

$\frac{6}{8}$ is thus duple compound meter (two beats, each divided into three parts). $\frac{9}{8}$ (triple compound meter with three dotted quarter beats) and $\frac{12}{8}$ (quadruple compound meter with four dotted quarter beats) are also compound meters, but $\frac{6}{8}$ is the most commonly used and the one we will focus on here.

As with the other meters we have studied, many different rhythmic patterns are possible in $\frac{6}{8}$. There are two beats in the measure: The first beat is the downbeat, the second is the upbeat.

A measure of $\frac{6}{8}$ has the same duration as a measure of $\frac{3}{4}$. They are both the length of six eighth notes, but they are divided differently: a measure of $\frac{6}{8}$ consists of two beats, each a dotted quarter note long, while a measure of $\frac{3}{4}$ consists of three beats, each a quarter note long.

$\frac{6}{8}$ and $\frac{3}{4}$

Note that beams are used to define the beat: they never span across the division between beat 1 and beat 2.

Correct   Incorrect

Beams in $\frac{6}{8}$

As with beams, rests should be used to clarify the beats; a rest should not span across the division between beat 1 and beat 2.

Rests in $^6_8$

Correct   Incorrect

Conducting pattern

The **conducting pattern** for $^6_8$ is the same as for the other duple meters, $^2_4$ and $^2_2$ (see Lesson 10).

finished

Lesson 12: In-class activities

1. **Dictation.** Within each group, the instructor will perform the three rhythms in a random order. identify the rhythm you hear and tap it back.

Group 1   Group 2

a.   a.

b.   b.

c.   c.

Group 3

a.

b.

c.

2. **Solo.** Suggestions for performance: (1) another member of the class claps the beats (or just the downbeat of each measure) while you clap or tap the given rhythm; (2) stamp your foot on each downbeat while clapping the rhythm, or tapping it, or chanting it using the syllable "ta"; (3) tap the two beats of the measure with your hand while chanting the rhythm using the syllable "ta"; (4) say the beats of the measure (1-2) while tapping the rhythm with your hand; (5) tap the beats with one hand while tapping the rhythm with the other; (6) conduct the beats with your right hand while chanting the rhythm using the syllable "ta." It is a good idea to tap two preparatory beats, or count 1-2, or conduct one preparatory measure before beginning each exercise in order to establish the tempo.

a. **Allegro**

b. ♩. = 60

c. **Presto**

d. **Andante**

   e. Bach, Fugue in G Major (measures 1 and 4 have the same rhythm, as do measures 2 and 3).

   f. Mozart, Sonata (the rhythms in measures 1–3 are repeated in measures 5–7).

Andante grazioso

3. Duets. Suggestions for performance: (1) one student or group of students performs each part of the duet, either tapping or chanting "ta." Then switch parts; (2) a single student chants the higher rhythm while tapping the lower and then vice versa.

a.

b.

c.

d. Bach, Fugue in G Major (the two parts are rhythmically distinct—they rarely do the same thing at the same time).

e. Mozart, Sonata (as in the Bach Fugue, the two parts are rhythmically quite independent of each other).

4. Improvisation. You are given two measures of a rhythm in $\frac{6}{8}$. Continue and conclude by improvising two more measures. In your improvisation, use the rhythmic values and ideas found in the two measures you are given. Perform your improvisation by clapping your hands, tapping on your desk, or chanting using the syllable "ta." Three suggestions for performance: (1) improvise a two-measure continuation and conclusion; (2) perform your improvisation in continuing succession with other students, in tempo and without missing a beat. As one student concludes an improvisation, another begins immediately, either by performing all four measures (beginning with the two given measures) or just his or her two-measure improvisation; (3) after you complete an improvisation, another student may be asked to perform what he or she heard you do. The example that follows shows three possible continuations for a given opening.

Name: _____

Date: _____

Instructor's Name: _____

LESSON 12: EXERCISES

12-1. Insert barlines to create complete measures in $\frac{6}{8}$ meter.

12-2. There are blank places, indicated with arrows, in some of these measures in $\frac{6}{8}$ meter. Fill them in by adding one or more notes of the proper time-value.

12-3. Continue and complete the following short rhythmic compositions. Each should be four measures in length. Be prepared to perform your compositions in class.

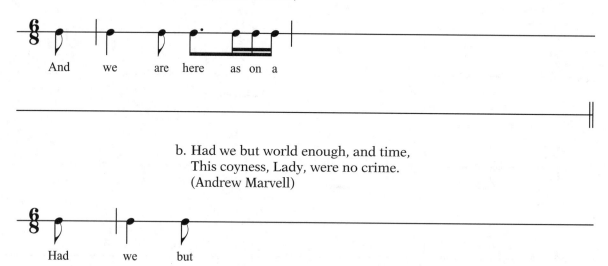

mysearchlab   12-4. Set the following poetic texts to an appropriate rhythm. Each syllable should receive a note. Accented syllables should be placed in accented parts of the measure; unaccented syllables should be placed in unaccented parts of the measure. You should write complete, correct measures in $^6_8$. Each setting is begun for you. Use as many measures as you feel you need. Be prepared to perform your settings in class. (See Exercise 6-4 for an example of the proper procedure.)

Note: In vocal music, composers traditionally use a separate stem and flag for each syllable of text, without beams; this practice can be seen throughout the anthology. In the written exercises, however, students are asked (at the discretion of the instructor) to use beams in the manner of instrumental music.

a. And we are here as on a darkling plain
   Swept with confused alarms of struggle and flight,
   Where ignorant armies clash by night.
   (Matthew Arnold)

And   we   are   here   as on a

b. Had we but world enough, and time,
   This coyness, Lady, were no crime.
   (Andrew Marvell)

Had   we   but

Lesson 13: Syncopation

In this lesson you will learn about syncopation, accent marks, ties, and subdivision.

Every meter has a fixed pattern of downbeats and upbeats, consisting of relatively accented and unaccented beats. And the beats themselves are divided into smaller units that are also either relatively accented or unaccented. **Syncopation** involves the contradiction of these underlying patterns. It makes the strong beats feel weak and the weak beats strong. In $\frac{4}{4}$ meter, for example, the first and third beats are relatively strong, while the second and fourth are relatively weak. This basic metrical framework may be contradicted in three ways:

Syncopation

recognize it!

1. A stress is placed on a weak beat by playing the note on that beat louder than normal. Often, composers use an **accent mark** to tell performers to place stress on a particular note.

Accent mark

Accent mark

2. A weak beat is tied to a strong beat. As a result, the weak beat receives a musical attack, but no note is attacked on a strong beat.

Ties

weak beat → strong beat = tie.

✗ strong beat → weak beat is NOT syncopation!

3. A strong beat is omitted, replaced by a rest.

Rests

Syncopations can occur in any meter. And they can occur both among the beats and among the **subdivisions** of the beats into accented and unaccented eighth notes.

Subdivision

Syncopations

Lesson 13: In-class activities

1. Dictation. Within each group, the instructor will perform the three rhythms in a random order. Identify the rhythm you hear and tap it back.

2. Solo. Suggestions for performance: (1) another member of the class claps the beats (or just the downbeat of each measure) while you clap or tap the given rhythm; (2) stamp your foot on each downbeat while clapping the rhythm, or tapping it, or chanting it using the syllable "ta"; (3) tap the beats with your hand while chanting the rhythm using the syllable "ta"; (4) say the beats of the measure while tapping the rhythm with your hand; (5) tap the beats with one hand while tapping the rhythm with the other; (6) conduct the beats with your right hand while chanting the rhythm using the syllable "ta." It is a good idea to tap preparatory beats, or count aloud, or conduct one preparatory measure before beginning each exercise in order to establish the tempo.

c. Joplin, "The Entertainer" (sixteenth notes are often joined to obscure the eighth-note beats).

d. Ellington, "It Don't Mean a Thing" (in measures 12, 14, and 16, there is a tie into the third beat of the measure).

e. Handy, "St. Louis Blues" (in the first measure, a tie is used into the third beat).

3. **Duets.** Suggestions for performance: (1) one student or group of students performs each part of the duet, either tapping or chanting "ta." Then switch parts; (2) a single student chants the higher rhythm while tapping the lower and then vice versa.

d. Ellington, "It Don't Mean a Thing" (the lower part provides a steady background for the intensive syncopations in the upper part).

e. Joplin, "The Entertainer" (the lower part moves in steady eighth notes against which the upper part provides nearly constant syncopations).

4. Improvisation. You are given two measures of syncopated rhythm in various meters. Continue and conclude by improvising two more measures. In your improvisation, use the rhythmic values and ideas found in the two measures you are given. Perform your improvisation by clapping your hands, tapping on your desk, or chanting using the syllable "ta." Three suggestions for performance: (1) improvise a two-measure continuation and conclusion; (2) perform your improvisation in continuing succession with other students, in tempo and without missing a beat. As one student concludes an improvisation, another begins immediately, either by performing all four measures (beginning with the two given measures) or just his or her two-measure improvisation; (3) after you complete an improvisation, another student may be asked to perform what he or she heard you do. The example that follows shows three possible continuations for a given opening.

Name: _____

Date: _____

Instructor's Name: _____

Lesson 13: Exercises

13-1. Syncopate these rhythms by adding ties and accents.

13-2. Continue and complete the following short rhythmic compositions. Each should be four measures in length. Use ties, rests, and accents to create syncopations. (Notating a syncopation occasionally involves obscuring a beat of the measure, as in the common pattern in the first measure of Exercise 13-2a.) Be prepared to perform your compositions in class.

13-3. Set the following poetic texts to an appropriate rhythm. Each syllable should receive a note. Use syncopations, which will deliberately distort the natural accentuation of the words. Each setting is begun for you. Use as many measures as you feel you need. Be prepared to perform your settings in class. (See Exercise 6-4 for an example of the proper procedure.)

Note: In vocal music, composers traditionally use a separate stem and flag for each syllable of text, without beams; this practice can be seen throughout the anthology at the end of this book. In the written exercises, however, students are asked (at the discretion of the instructor) to use beams in the manner of instrumental music.

a. I placed a jar in Tennessee,
   And round it was, upon a hill.
   (Wallace Stevens)

b. With his ebony hands on each ivory key
   He made that poor piano moan with melody.
   (Langston Hughes)

Chapter 2: Supplementary Lesson

In this lesson you will learn about rhythmic values smaller than a sixteenth note, triplets, and other duple, triple, and quadruple meters.

The hierarchy of note values discussed in previous lessons—whole note, half note, quarter note, eighth note, sixteenth note—can be extended downward to notes of even shorter duration. A **thirty-second note** is half as long as a sixteenth note, and is written with a triple flag or beam. A **sixty-fourth note** is half as long as a thirty-second note, and is written with a quadruple flag or beam.

Thirty-second note
Sixty-fourth note

Whole note

Half note

Quarter note

Eighth note

Sixteenth note

Thirty-second note

Sixty-fourth note   etc.   etc.

These basic note values, together with augmentation dots and ties, provide a rich variety of possible durations.

One additional kind of note value is a **triplet**, which is used to divide into *three* parts a note that is normally divided in *two*. A quarter note, for example, is usually divided into two eighth notes, but can be divided instead into an **eighth-note triplet.**

Triplet

Eighth-note triplet

instead of

In the same way, a whole note can be divided into a **half-note triplet**; a half note can be divided into a **quarter-note triplet**; and an eighth note can be divided into a **sixteenth-note triplet.**

Half-note triplets		instead of	
Quarter-note triplets		instead of	
Eighth-note triplets		instead of	
Sixteenth-note triplets		instead of	

In previous lessons, we focused on the most commonly used musical meters: $\frac{4}{4}$ (or $\mathbf{c}$), $\frac{2}{2}$ (or $\mathbf{\phi}$), $\frac{2}{4}$, $\frac{3}{4}$, and $\frac{6}{8}$. Other meters are also in occasional use. Here are the main possibilities:

	Time value of the beat	Duple meter 2 beats per measure	Triple meter 3 beats per measure	Quadruple meter 4 beats per measure
Simple	Half note	$\frac{2}{2}$ or $\mathbf{\phi}$	$\frac{3}{2}$	$\frac{4}{2}$
	Quarter note	$\frac{2}{4}$	$\frac{3}{4}$	$\frac{4}{4}$ or $\mathbf{c}$
	Eighth note	$\frac{2}{8}$	$\frac{3}{8}$	$\frac{4}{8}$
Compound	Dotted half note	$\frac{6}{4}$	$\frac{9}{4}$	$\frac{12}{4}$
	Dotted quarter note	$\frac{6}{8}$	$\frac{9}{8}$	$\frac{12}{8}$
	Dotted eighth note	$\frac{6}{16}$	$\frac{9}{16}$	$\frac{12}{16}$

Chapter 2: Self-Test

There are blank spots in some of these measures (indicated by arrows). Fill them in by inserting one (1) note of the proper time-value.

Chapter 2: Self-Test (answer key)

3 Major and Minor Scales

Lesson 14: Major scale (C major)

In this lesson you will learn about the major scale, its arrangement of semitones and whole tones, scale-degree numbers, scale-degree names, and solfège syllables.

A **scale** is a collection of notes used for a musical composition or part of a composition. The notes are extracted from the music and written in ascending order, within an octave. There are two scales commonly used in tonal music: **major** and **minor.** In major and minor scales, each letter name occurs once; none is omitted and none occurs more than once (except the first note, which is duplicated at the octave). Major and minor scales thus contain seven different notes.

Scale

Major scale
Minor scale

A **semitone (ST)** is the smallest possible space between two notes. On the piano keyboard, any two adjacent keys are a semitone apart. Twelve semitones make up an octave.

Semitone

Semitones

The note D, for example, lies a semitone above C♯ and a semitone below E♭. Similarly, F is a semitone above E and a semitone below G♭.

Two semitones make up a **whole tone (WT).** Two notes a whole tone apart are separated by one intervening note. A whole tone consists of two notes with different letter names, written on a space and the adjacent line (or vice versa).

Whole tone

Whole tones

Among the white notes, C–D, D–E, F–G, G–A, and A–B are whole tones (they all have a black note separating them).

A major scale consists of a particular sequence of whole tones and semitones above any given note: whole tone, whole tone, semitone, whole tone, whole tone, whole tone, semitone. A C major scale involves that sequence written starting on C—it is the only major scale that can be written without any accidentals.

C major scale

WT   WT   ST   WT   WT   WT   ST   *always same order!*

121

Scale degree

Each note of the scale is called a **scale degree** and these are commonly numbered $\hat{1}$ through $\hat{8}$, with scale-degree $\hat{8}$ the same as scale-degree $\hat{1}$ an octave higher. Scale-degree numbers are designated by a caret (^) over the number.

F♯ major scale degree 1 = F♯!

^ ← little hat!

Scale-degree numbers

There are semitones between scale-degrees $\hat{3}$–$\hat{4}$ and $\hat{7}$–$\hat{8}$. All the other steps in the scale are whole tones.

Tonic
Supertonic
Mediant
Subdominant
Dominant
Submediant
Leading tone

Scale degrees are also called by the names **tonic, supertonic, mediant, subdominant, dominant, submediant,** and **leading tone.**

tendency notes: not 1, 3, 5 notes. wants to go to 1, 3, or 5.

Scale-degree names

The tonic lies at the center of this naming system, with the mediant and dominant three and five steps above, and the submediant and subdominant three and five steps below.

central to the

Tonic, in the middle

| subdominant | submediant | tonic | mediant | dominant |

5 steps   3 steps   3 steps   5 steps

SKIP not useful for our course

Solfège syllables
Do
Re
Mi
Fa
Sol
La
Ti

The scale degrees are also sometimes referred to with **solfège syllables**: **do** (pronounced "doh"), **re** (pronounced "ray"), **mi** (pronounced "mee"), **fa** (pronounced "fah"), **sol** (pronounced "soh"), **la** (pronounced "lah"), and **ti** (pronounced "tee"). These syllables are commonly used when music is sung.

Solfège syllables

do   re   mi   fa   sol   la   ti   do

We thus have three different ways of naming each note of the C major scale:

Note	Scale-degree number	Scale-degree name	Solfège syllable
C	$\hat{1}$ or $\hat{8}$	Tonic	*do*
D	$\hat{2}$	Supertonic	*re*
E	$\hat{3}$	Mediant	*mi*
F	$\hat{4}$	Subdominant	*fa*
G	$\hat{5}$	Dominant	*sol*
A	$\hat{6}$	Submediant	*la*
B	$\hat{7}$	Leading tone	*ti*

Each degree of the scale has its own distinctive character, its own dynamic quality and tendencies.

Dynamic qualities

The tonic (scale-degree $\hat{1}$) embodies a sense of poised repose—it is normally both the origin and goal of melodic motion, and the other degrees of the scale tend to move toward it. It is the principal scale degree. The dominant (scale-degree $\hat{5}$) is the second most important and stable scale degree. It lies just beyond the midpoint of the scale and can be pulled either upward or downward to the tonic. The supertonic (scale-degree $\hat{2}$), so called because it is a step above the tonic, is often pulled down one step toward the tonic, as though caught in a gravitational pull. The mediant (scale-degree $\hat{3}$), so called because it is halfway between the tonic and the dominant, is relatively stable compared to the supertonic. Melodic motion often passes downward from the mediant to the tonic via the supertonic. The subdominant (scale-degree $\hat{4}$) tends to move downward to the more stable mediant, a semitone below it. The submediant (scale-degree $\hat{6}$) is pulled downward toward the dominant, a step below it. The leading tone (scale-degree $\hat{7}$) is so called because it has such a strong tendency to move upward to the relatively stable tonic, a semitone above it. In short, the major scale is not a neutral bunch of notes but a scene of dynamism and activity. It is a network of relations in which each scale degree has a distinctive character and role.

Lesson 14: In-class activities

1. **Singing.** Sing these three-note melodic fragments using scale-degree numbers, solfège syllables, or a neutral syllable like "la," as indicated by your instructor.

2. **Singing.** Sing these melodies using scale-degree numbers, solfège syllables, or a neutral syllable like "la," as indicated by your instructor.

3. **Singing.** Sing these melodies using scale-degree numbers, solfège syllables, or a neutral syllable like "la," as indicated by your instructor.

   a. Mozart, "Dove sono" (adapted; the melody starts in measure 9 as it did at the beginning, but diverges thereafter).

   b. Haydn, String Quartet.

4. **Singing (improvise).** Continue and conclude the following short melodies (each should last four measures). Use only the notes of the C major scale, and use only whole notes, half notes, and quarter notes. Sing using scale-degree numbers, solfège syllables, or a neutral syllable like "la," as indicated by your instructor. You may perform your improvisation in continuing succession with other students, in tempo and without missing a beat. As one student concludes an improvisation, another begins immediately, starting with the two given measures and concluding with his or her own two-measure improvisation.

5. Singing (improvise). You are given a melody in whole notes. Using only the notes of the C major scale, elaborate and decorate that melody using the suggested rhythmic values. Each improvisation is begun for you.

1) Given melody

2) Half notes only

3) Quarter notes only

4) Half notes and quarter notes

6. Singing (duets). Two students or groups of students sing the two lines of the following duets. Then switch parts. Sing using scale-degree numbers, solfège syllables, or a neutral syllable like "la," as indicated by your instructor.

a.   b.   c.   d.

e.   f.   g.

7. Dictation. The instructor will play a C major scale to establish a context and then will play a series of individual notes from the scale. Sing the note back with the correct scale-degree number or solfège syllable. The instructor will begin with C, E, and G only, then gradually add the remaining four notes.

8. Dictation. Within each group the instructor will play melodic patterns in a random order. Identify the pattern being played and then sing it back, either on a neutral syllable like "la" or using scale-degree numbers or solfège syllables.

9. Playing. Learn to play a C major scale in one octave with your right hand alone and with your left hand alone (fingerings are provided).

10. Playing. Learn to play these melodies with your right hand and then, transposed an octave lower, with your left hand (fingerings provided).

a. Mozart, "Dove sono"

b. Haydn, String Quartet

11. Playing (improvise). In-class activities 4 and 5 (on pp. 124–126) involve improvisation. Instead of singing, perform your improvisations on the piano.

Name: _____

Date: _____

Instructor's Name: _____

LESSON 14: EXERCISES

14-1. Within the C major scale, identify these notes with scale-degree numbers, scale-degree names, and solfège syllables, as indicated.

a. scale-degree numbers

b. scale-degree names

c. solfège syllables

14-2. Within the C major scale, identify these notes with scale-degree numbers.

a. Haydn, String Quartet (this melody features large leaps).

b. Mozart, "Dove sono" (in the first two measures, scale-degree $\hat{1}$ is surrounded by notes directly above and below it. The same thing happens to scale-degree $\hat{3}$ in measures 3–4).

c. Joplin, "The Entertainer" (the two lines here are actually a single melody played in octaves. Ignore the note in parentheses—it does not belong to the C major scale, but fills the space between $\hat{6}$ and $\hat{5}$).

mysearchlab   14-3. Compose a melody for each of these texts. If you wish, you may use the rhythms you previously composed for these texts in Exercise 6-4. Use only the notes of the C major scale and remember the dynamic tendencies of the scale degrees. Use only whole notes, half notes, and quarter notes. Each melody is begun for you. Play your melodies on the piano or other instrument before handing them in—be sure they sound the way you want them to. Be prepared to sing your melodies in class.

a. Do not go gentle into that good night.
   Rage, rage against the dying of the light.
   (Dylan Thomas)

Name: _____

Date: _____

Instructor's Name: _____

b. When in disgrace with fortune and men's eyes,
   I all alone beweep my outcast state.
   (William Shakespeare)

14-4. Fill in the blanks in these melodies by adding whatever notes from the C major scale sound best to you (bearing in mind the dynamic tendencies of the different scale degrees). Use only whole notes, half notes, and quarter notes. Play your melodies on the piano or other instrument before handing them in—be sure they sound the way you want them to. Be prepared to sing your melodies in class.

Lesson 15: Major scales other than C major

In this lesson you will learn about transposition, major scales with sharps, major scales with flats, and the circle of fifths.

A scale is named for its tonic (scale-degree $\hat{1}$). The major scale discussed in Lesson 14 has the note C as its tonic and is thus called a C major scale. But any note can be the tonic of a major scale. We simply **transpose** the scale to start on a different note, preserving its internal structure. To do so, however, requires the use of accidentals (sharps or flats). To write a G major scale, for example, requires an F♯.

Transposition

G major scale

Without the F♯, there would be two steps of the wrong size: a semitone between scale-degrees $\hat{6}$ and $\hat{7}$ and a whole tone between scale-degrees $\hat{7}$ and $\hat{8}$ The F♯ makes all of the steps the correct size.

To write a major scale starting on D requires sharping both the F and the C.

D major scale

The C major scale requires no sharps or flats. The G major scale, which begins on scale-degree $\hat{5}$ of C major, requires one sharp (F♯). The D major scale, which begins on scale-degree $\hat{5}$ of G major, requires two sharps (F♯ and C♯). Every time we transpose up five steps in this way, an additional sharp is required. Notice that the sharps are added in a particular order: F♯–C♯–G♯–D♯–A♯–E♯–B♯. Like the tonics of the scales that use sharps, the sharps themselves ascend five steps each time. (When counting the number of steps, be sure to include the note you start on. So, for example, from C to G is five steps—C, D, E, F, G).

Major scales with sharps

Something similar happens moving downward by five steps. To write an F major scale, of which C is scale-degree $\hat{5}$ requires one flat (B♭).

F major scale

To write a B♭ major scale, of which F is scale-degree $\hat{5}$ requires two flats (B♭ and E♭).

B♭ major scale

Every time we transpose down five steps, an additional flat is required. Notice that the flats are added in a certain order: B♭–E♭–A♭–D♭–G♭–C♭–F♭. Like the tonics of the scales that use flats, the flats themselves descend five steps each time.

Major scales with flats

If we start on C and move up five steps at a time in one direction and down five steps at a time in the other, we will eventually meet back in the middle, creating a **circle of fifths** on which all of the major scales and the accidentals needed to make them can be conveniently listed. (A fifth is the space between two notes that span five steps, like C and G, which span C–D–E–F–G.)

Circle of fifths

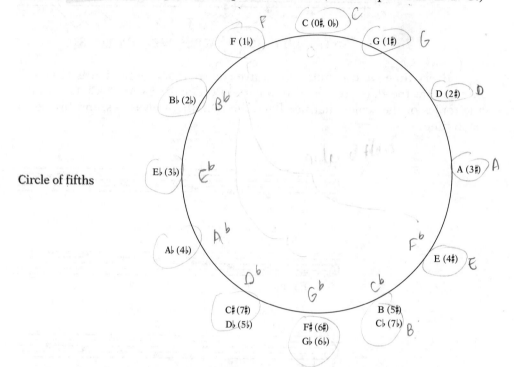

Circle of fifths

Enharmonic equivalence

Because of **enharmonic equivalence,** some scales are listed twice. G♭ major, for example, has six flats, while F♯ major has six sharps. The two scales are played with exactly the same notes on the keyboard, but are spelled differently.

The circle of fifths is the basic structure in relating major scales because the major scale is itself made up of fifths. Any major scale can be understood as a series of seven adjacent notes in the circle of fifths. Here are the notes of the C major scale identified as a contiguous segment of the circle of fifths.

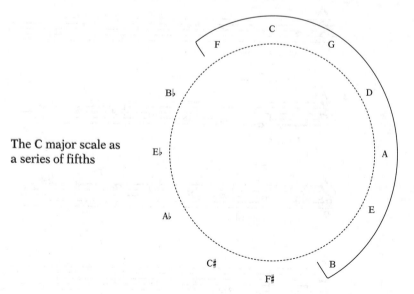

The C major scale as a series of fifths

→ 16.

Transposing that scale up by fifth involves shifting it one notch around clockwise. F is omitted while F♯ is added, and now we have the notes of the G major scale.

Circle of Fifths (#s order):
Father Charles Goes Down And
Ends Battle

FCGDAEB

Flats:
Battle Ends And Down
Goes Charles Father

(order you write key signatures on clef)

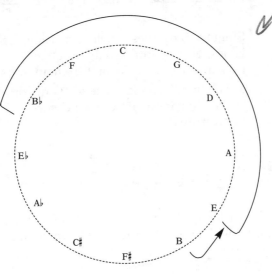

From C major to G major

From C major to F major

Each transposition of a major scale upward by fifth works in just this way, shifting one notch clockwise around the circle of fifths, and thus adding sharps in the prescribed order.

Transposing down by fifth involves shifting one notch counterclockwise around the circle of fifths. When C major is transposed down a fifth to F major, for example, B is omitted while B♭ is added.

Each downward transposition by five steps shifts the collection of notes one notch counterclockwise on the circle of fifths and thus adds flats in the prescribed order.

Lesson 15: In-class activities

1. **Singing.** Sing the following common five-note patterns (given in D major and B♭ major). Sing using scale-degree numbers, solfège syllables, or a neutral syllable such as "la," as directed by your instructor.

2. **Singing.** Sing these melodies using scale-degree numbers, solfège syllables, or a neutral syllable such as "la," as directed by your instructor. Remember that accidentals remain in force throughout a measure.

   a. Schubert, "Heidenröslein" (G major; the melody moves down toward the tonic in the first two measures, then up to the tonic in the last two measures).

   b. Mendelssohn, Piano Trio (adapted, D major; the melody creates spaces with upward leaps and fills them in with downward steps).

c. Bach, Fugue in G Major (it takes three measures for the melody to ascend from G4 to D5 and a single measure to get back to its starting point).

d. Mozart, Sonata (A major; measures 5–8 begin the same as measures 1–4 but end differently).

3. **Singing (improvise).** Continue and conclude the following short melodies (each should last four measures). Use only the notes of the G major scale (for the first melody) and the B♭ major scale (for the second melody), and use only whole notes, half notes, quarter notes, and eighth notes. Sing using scale-degree numbers, solfège syllables, or a neutral syllable like "la," as indicated by your instructor. You may perform your improvisation in continuing succession with other students, in tempo and without missing a beat. As one student concludes an improvisation, another begins immediately, starting with the two given measures and concluding with his or her own two-measure improvisation.

4. **Singing (improvise).** You are given a melody in whole notes. Using only the notes of the appropriate major scale (G major for the first melody, B♭ major for the second, and D major for the third), elaborate and decorate that melody using the suggested rhythmic values. Each improvisation is begun for you.

1) Given melody

2) Half notes and quarter notes

5. Singing (duets). Two students or groups of students sing the two lines of the following duets. Then switch parts. Sing using scale-degree numbers, solfège syllables, or a neutral syllable like "la," as indicated by your instructor.

6. Dictation. Within each group, the instructor will play the scales in a random order. Identify the scale played as major or nonmajor. Only one scale in each group is major.

7. Playing. You are given a note and told its scale degree. Play the appropriate major scale down to its tonic, then up through an octave.

8. Playing (improvise). You are given a note and told its scale degree. Starting with that note, improvise a short melody that ends on the tonic of the appropriate major scale. The melody should be in $\frac{4}{4}$ and use only whole notes, half notes, quarter notes, and eighth notes.

9. Playing. Learn to play major scales in one octave with each hand alone and with both hands together. Here are the recommended fingerings for the major scales that use three or fewer accidentals.

Name: _____

Date: _____

Instructor's Name: _____

LESSON 15: EXERCISES

15-1. Write major scales by adding the appropriate sharps or flats (major scales with three or fewer accidentals). Remember to write each accidental directly before the note it modifies.

15-2. Write major scales by adding the appropriate sharps or flats (all major scales). Remember to write each accidental directly before the note it modifies.

15-3. You are given a note and told what scale degree it is. Write the appropriate major scale (scales with three or fewer accidentals).

Name: _____

Date: _____

Instructor's Name: _____

15-4. You are given a note and told what scale degree it is. Write the appropriate major scale (all major scales).

B♭ major

a. E is $\hat{4}$ D is $\hat{3}$

b. D♯ is $\hat{2}$ C♯ major   C♯ is $\hat{7}$ D major (FC)

c. C is $\hat{5}$ F major   B♭ is $\hat{5}$

d. F♯ is $\hat{6}$ F is $\hat{4}$

e. C is $\hat{7}$ G♯ is $\hat{3}$

f. A is $\hat{2}$ G major   C is $\hat{3}$ A♭ major   4♭'s (BEAD)

g. E♭ is $\hat{6}$ E♯ is $\hat{7}$

mysearchlab

15-5. You are given the name of a major scale and a scale degree. Write the appropriate note (scales with three or fewer accidentals).

mysearchlab

15-6. You are given the name of a major scale and a scale degree. Write the appropriate note (all major scales).

Name: _____

Date: _____

Instructor's Name: _____

15-7. In each of these passages, identify the major scale used by writing it in the appropriate space beneath the score. Remember that accidentals remain in force throughout a measure.

a. Chopin, Prelude (disregard the B♯ and D♯ in measure 3—they decorate the C♯ and E they precede).

C♯, G♯ F♯

A major

b. Schubert, "Heidenröslein" (the song begins with one major scale, moves to another, then returns to its starting point. Disregard the A♯ in measure 9—it decorates the B before and after it).

F, C

D major (2 sharps)

war so jung und mor - gen-schön,   lief er schnell es   nah' zu — sehn,   sah's mit vie - len   Freu - den.
it was so fresh and   beau - ti - ful   he ran quickly to   gaze at — it,   gaze   with   great — joy.

FL -

Rös-lein, Rös - lein,   Rös - lein — roth,   Rös - lein auf der   Hei - den.
Lit - tle rose, —   little red — rose,   rose — amid the   hea - ther.

c. Schumann, Song (this song begins with one major scale then moves
to another. Disregard the B♭ in measure 5).

G major

Wenn ich in dei - ne   Au - gen seh',   so   schwin - det all' mein   Leid und
When I in - to your   eyes — look,   then   fades — all   my   pain and

Name: _____

Date: _____

Instructor's Name: _____

15-8. Transpose these melodies as requested. When you transpose a melody, you start on a different note and proceed in a different key, but maintain the shape, internal structure (including all semitones and whole tones), and sound of the original. Transposition from one key to another always requires the use of accidentals (sharps or flats). Play your work on a piano or other instrument before handing it in—be sure it sounds the way you want it to.

a. Mozart, "Dove sono"

b. Haydn, String Quartet

c. Arlen, "Over the Rainbow"

15-9. Compose a melody for each of these texts. If you wish, you may use the rhythms you previously composed for these texts in Exercise 7-5. The first melody should use the notes of the D major scale; the second melody should use the notes of the F major scale. Use only whole notes, half notes, quarter notes, and eighth notes. Each melody is begun for you. Play your melodies on the piano or other instrument before handing them in—be sure they sound the way you want them to. Be prepared to sing your melodies in class.

a. Whither is fled the visionary gleam?
   Where is it now, the glory and the dream?
   (William Wordsworth)

Name: _____

Date: _____

Instructor's Name: _____

b. Let us go then, you and I,
   When the evening is spread out against the sky
   Like a patient etherized upon a table.
   (T. S. Eliot)

Let   us   go   then,   you   and

15-10. Fill in the blanks in these melodies by adding whatever notes from the B♭ major scale (first melody) and G major scale (second melody) sound best to you (bearing in mind the dynamic tendencies of the different scale degrees). Use only whole notes, half notes, quarter notes, and eighth notes. Play your melodies on the piano or other instrument before handing them in—be sure they sound the way you want them to. Be prepared to sing your melodies in class.

scale degrees: 1-8
tonic key = name of the scale

Lesson 16: Major keys and key signatures

1. circle of fifths (memorize)

C G 1# D 2# CGDAEB A 3# E 4# B 5#
Bb F Eb Ab Db Gb Cb F# B
CGDAEBCF Db Gb Cb FAB

In this lesson you will learn about major keys and key signatures.

Each major scale embodies a distinctive network of relationships. Each contains its own unique tonic, its own unique supertonic, its own unique mediant, and so on. Two major scales may have as many as six notes in common, but no two scales contain all of the same notes. Every major scale contains one and only one statement of each of the seven letter names (A, B, C, D, E, F, G)—only the accidentals vary, but this variety is enough to distinguish the scales from each other.

2. memorize FCGDAEB mnemonic for key signatures

Scale-degree Name Syllable	$\hat{1}$ tonic *do*	$\hat{2}$ supertonic *re*	$\hat{3}$ mediant *mi*	$\hat{4}$ subdominant *fa*	$\hat{5}$ dominant *sol*	$\hat{6}$ submediant *la*	$\hat{7}$ leading tone *ti*
C major	C	D	E	F	G	A	B
G major	G	A	B	C	D	E	F♯
D major	D	E	F♯	G	A	B	C♯
A major	A	B	C♯	D	E	F♯	G♯
E major	E	F♯	G♯	A	B	C♯	D♯
B major	B	C♯	D♯	E	F♯	G♯	A♯
C♭ major	C♭	D♭	E♭	F♭	G♭	A♭	B♭
F♯ major	F♯	G♯	A♯	B	C♯	D♯	E♯
G♭ major	G♭	A♭	B♭	C♭	D♭	E♭	F
C♯ major	C♯	D♯	E♯	F♯	G♯	A♯	B♯
D♭ major	D♭	E♭	F	G♭	A♭	B♭	C
A♭ major	A♭	B♭	C	D♭	E♭	F	G
E♭ major	E♭	F	G	A♭	B♭	C	D
B♭ major	B♭	C	D	E♭	F	G	A
F major	F	G	A	B♭	C	D	E

This network of relationships within each scale is what defines a **key**. A piece is in the key of D major, for example, if it begins and ends by using the notes of the D major scale and treats D as tonic, A as dominant, C♯ as leading tone, and so on. In pieces that are based on a particular major scale, it would be possible just to write the necessary accidentals each time they are called for, but this would be cumbersome. Instead, the necessary accidentals are *simply written* at the beginning of each line of the piece, right after the clef, in a **key signature.**

Key

Key signature

The A major scale, for example, uses three sharps: F♯, C♯, and G♯. Instead of writing sharp signs in front of every F, C, and G in a piece, composers just write the appropriate key signature, and all of the Fs, Cs, and Gs are automatically sharped.

This:

Key signature

Instead of this:

The accidentals in the key signature need to be written in the proper place on the staff and in the proper order. The key of C major has a key signature of no sharps and no flats. The key of G major uses one sharp, namely F♯, and a sharp sign is placed accordingly on the top line of the treble staff and the fourth line of the bass staff.

G major

That key signature indicates that every time the note F appears, in any octave, it will be played as F♯ (unless a natural sign is used temporarily to cancel it).

Shifting to a tonic five steps higher, the key of D major uses two sharps: F♯ and C♯. Sharp signs are accordingly placed on the top line of the treble and the fourth line of the bass staff (these sharp all of the Fs) and on the third space of the treble and the second space of the bass staff (these sharp all of the Cs).

D major

Moving another five steps higher, A major uses three sharps: F♯, C♯, and G♯.

A major

Keys with flats in their signature work the same way. The key of F major, five steps below C, has a signature of one flat: B♭. Five steps below F, the key of B♭ major has a signature of two flats: B♭ and E♭. Five steps below B♭, the key of E♭ major has a signature of three flats: B♭, E♭, and A♭. As with sharps, these accidentals are written on particular lines or spaces of the treble and bass staves and apply throughout a piece in all octaves.

Major keys
with flats

The key signatures for all of the major keys can be written conveniently around the circle of fifths.

Major key
signatures

Each time you move clockwise, you add a sharp (or take away a flat). Each time you move counterclockwise, you add a flat (or take away a sharp). Notice that the sharps and flats accumulate in a particular order: F♯–C♯–G♯–D♯–A♯–E♯–B♯ for sharps and the reverse, B♭–E♭–A♭–D♭–G♭–C♭–F♭, for flats.

Lesson 16: In-class activities

1. **Singing.** Sing the following common seven-note patterns (given in G major and F major). Sing using scale-degree numbers, solfège syllables, or a neutral syllable such as "la," as directed by your instructor.

2. **Singing.** Sing these melodies using scale-degree numbers, solfège syllables, or a neutral syllable such as "la," as directed by your instructor.

a. Arlen, "Over the Rainbow" (the melody hovers in one place then ascends directly to the tonic).

b. Lang, Song (the melody starts and ends on the same note, scale-
degree 3̂).

c. Mozart, Sonata (adapted; the melody ascends to a high A before ending on a low A).

d. Schubert, "Heidenröslein" (adapted; the melody begins with a simple
G major scale).

e. Schumann, Song (the melody descends B–A–G two times—the second
one sounds like a real ending).

3. Singing (improvise). Continue and conclude the following short
melodies (each should last four measures). The first melody is in D major
and the second is in G major. Use dotted rhythms and/or ties as appropriate. Sing using scale-degree numbers, solfège syllables, or a neutral
syllable like "la," as indicated by your instructor. You may perform your
improvisation in continuing succession with other students, in tempo
and without missing a beat. As one student concludes an improvisation,
another begins immediately, starting with the two given measures and
concluding with his or her own two-measure improvisation.

a.

b.

4. Singing (improvise). You are given a melody in whole notes. Using only the notes of the appropriate major key, elaborate and decorate that melody using the suggested rhythmic values. Each improvisation is begun for you.

1) Given melody

c.

2) Use dotted quarter notes

3) Use ties

4) Use dotted eighth notes

5. Singing (duets). Two students or groups of students sing the two lines of the following duets. Then switch parts. Sing using scale-degree numbers, solfège syllables, or a neutral syllable like "la," as indicated by your instructor.

6. Playing (improvise). You are given a key signature and a note. Starting with that note, improvise a short melody that ends on the tonic of the appropriate major key.

7. Playing. Learn to play the following five-finger pattern in all major keys. Play first with each hand alone and then with both hands together.

8. Playing. Learn to play the following five-finger pattern as it moves through all of the major keys. The last note of each pattern becomes the first note of the next. Alternate hands.

Name: _____

Date: _____

Instructor's Name: _____

LESSON 16: EXERCISES

16-1. Identify the major key represented by these key signatures (keys with three or fewer flats or sharps in the key signature).

16-2. Identify the major key represented by these key signatures (all keys).

d. F#   Eb   Gb   F   E

e. C#   Gb   F   G   Gb

f. D   Ab   C#   D   A

g. Bb   B   Cb   F#   F

16-3. Write the key signature for these major keys (keys with three or fewer accidentals in the key signature). Remember to write accidentals in the correct order and position on the staff (see circle of fifths diagram on p. 157 for models).

a. G   F   D   Eb   A   C   Bb

b. C   A   Bb   G   Eb   D   F

c. Eb   D   F   Bb   G   C   A

16-4. Write the key signature for these major keys (all keys). Remember to write accidentals in the correct order and position on the staff (see circle of fifths diagram on p. 157 for models).

a. B   G 1#   Eb 3b   D 2#   F 1#   E 4#

b. A 3#   Ab 4b   C   Gb 6b 6's   F# C#   Db 5b

Name: _____

Date: _____

Instructor's Name: _____

c.

Gb 6b   F# 6#   Cb 7b   Bb 2b   B 5#   C# 7#

d.

B 5#   D 2#   F 1b   E 4#   Bb 2b   G 1#

e.

Eb 3b   A 3#   C# 7#   Ab 4b   C   Db 5b

16-5. Name the keys of these pieces.

  a. Joplin, "The Entertainer" (disregard the notes in parentheses—they
     do not belong to the key, but serve to decorate those that do).

D F
F C G D
e

Key: E maj

  b. Lang, Song (the bass note at the beginning and end of a phrase is
     often scale-degree as it is here).

3b = Eb

Langsam und Ausdrucksvoll (Slowly and expressively)

Ob ich manch-mal dein Ge - den - ke?   wüsst-est Du   wie sehr ich's thu!
Do   I   some-times think of you?_____   If   on - ly   you knew how much!

Key: Eb

c. Mozart, Sonata.

Key: ___A maj___

d. Schubert, "Heidenröslein" (as in the Lang song, the bass note at the beginning and end of the phrase provides scale-degree 1̂).

Key: ___G maj___

e. Chopin, Prelude (the B♯ and D♯ in measure 3 do not belong to the key—they decorate the C♯ and E to which they move).

Key: ___A maj___

Name: _____

Date: _____

Instructor's Name: _____

f. Arlen, "Over the Rainbow."

When all the world is a   hope-less jum-ble and the   rain-drops tum-ble all a - round,

Key: _____

g. Bach, Fugue.

Key: _Gmaj_

h. Bach, Chorale.

Key: _D maj_

i. Mozart, "Dove sono."

Do - ve so - no   i bei   mo - men - ti
I   re - mem - ber   days long   de - part - ed,

Key: _____

j. Mendelssohn, Piano Trio.

Key: _____

k. Schumann, Song.

Wenn ich in dei - ne Au - gen seh',   so   scwhin det all' mein Leid und Weh,

Key: _____

Name: _____

Date: _____

Instructor's Name: _____

16-6. Compose a melody for each of these texts. If you wish, you may use the rhythms you previously composed for these texts in Exercise 8-5. Use dotted rhythms as appropriate. Each melody is begun for you. Play your melodies on the piano or other instrument before handing them in—be sure they sound the way you want them to. Be prepared to sing your melodies in class.

a. O body swayed to music, O brightening glance,
   How can we know the dancer from the dance?
   (W. B. Yeats)

b. Because I could not stop for Death—
   He kindly stopped for me.
   (Emily Dickinson)

16-7. Fill in the blanks in these melodies by adding whatever notes from the appropriate major key sound best to you (bearing in mind the dynamic tendencies of the different scale degrees). Use dotted rhythms as appropriate. Play your melodies on the piano or other instrument before handing them in—be sure they sound the way you want them to. Be prepared to sing your melodies in class.

(natural)

C major & A minor = relative major & minor keys

(relationship): If start on scale degree 6 of a major, = corresponding
                                                        <u>NATURAL</u> <u>minor key</u>!!

eg. E major: relative = C# minor → natural has same accidentals
    (key sig.)

D' m   → relative ma

ex: D minor. D is scale deg. 6 of what maj scale?
    ↳ same key sig. as F! F is the relative major

ST in natural minor: 2⌢3 and 5⌢6
    ↳ can use this to build scale & put accidentals in!!

<u>2 ways</u> to find key sig. for minor scale

① relative maj/minor scales (finding) + using ST/WT placement/order

② memorizing circle of 5ths for both

E♭ major → minor = ?
↳ C = 6th note, C natural minor - 3♭'s

(handwritten top margin: ♯205 · relative keys chart = memorize this!!)

Lesson 17: Minor scale (A minor)

In this lesson you will learn about the minor scale, its arrangement of semitones and whole tones, scale-degree numbers, scale-degree names, solfège syllables, and raising scale-degrees $\hat{6}$ and $\hat{7}$.

Minor scale

The **minor scale** has a different arrangement of semitones and whole tones compared to the major scale. The minor scale has semitones between scale-degrees $\hat{2}$–$\hat{3}$ and $\hat{5}$–$\hat{6}$ while the major scale has semitones between scale-degrees $\hat{3}$–$\hat{4}$ and $\hat{7}$–$\hat{8}$. All other steps in the scale are whole tones. Like the C major scale, the A minor scale can be written without any accidentals.

Major and minor

(handwritten right margin: relative major/minor = same key signature, different tonic notes)

Scale degrees

As in major, the **scale degrees** have names as well as numbers: tonic, supertonic, mediant, subdominant, dominant, submediant, and subtonic.

Scale-degree numbers and names

Subtonic

Notice that scale-degree $\hat{7}$ in minor is called the **subtonic** rather than the **leading tone.** That is because it is a whole tone rather than a semitone below scale-degree $\hat{8}$, and thus lacks a sense of directed movement toward the tonic.

Solfège syllables

Musicians often use **solfège syllables** when singing melodies in minor. As in major, the syllable **do** is assigned to the tonic of the scale, **re** to the supertonic, and so on. Instead of **mi, la,** and **ti,** some musicians use **me** (pronounced "may"), **le** (pronounced "lay"), and **te** (pronounced "tay") for scale-degrees $\hat{3}$, $\hat{6}$ and $\hat{7}$ in minor.

We thus have three ways of naming the degrees of the minor scale: with numbers, names, and solfège syllables.

Do
Re
Me
Fa
Sol
Le
Te

Note	Scale-degree number	Scale-degree name	Solfège syllable
A	$\hat{1}$	Tonic	*do*
B	$\hat{2}$	Supertonic	*re*
C	$\hat{3}$	Mediant	*me* (*mi* in major)
D	$\hat{4}$	Subdominant	*fa*
E	$\hat{5}$	Dominant	*sol*
F	$\hat{6}$	Submediant	*le* (*la* in major)
G	$\hat{7}$	Subtonic	*te* (*ti* in major)

As with the degrees of the major scale, each degree of the minor scale has a distinctive dynamic character.

Dynamic qualities

As in the major, the tonic is the principal scale degree, with all melodic movement departing from and returning to it, and the dominant is the most important counterweight, dividing the scale nearly in half. The lack of a leading tone means that motions often descend from the tonic toward the dominant. There is a particularly strong pull downward from the submediant to the dominant, only a semitone below. Similarly, there is a strong pull from the mediant down through the supertonic (a semitone below) to the tonic. There is thus a strong downward pull, which lends the minor scale a darker, more brooding character than the major scale.

In writing music using the minor scale, composers often create a leading tone by raising the subtonic a semitone, making the note natural if it was flat, sharp if it was natural, and double sharp if it was sharp. Scale-degree $\hat{7}$ is now only a semitone below the tonic. When scale-degree $\hat{7}$ is raised in this way, it **Leading tone (ti)** is called a **leading tone** (rather than a subtonic) and is sung with the solfège syllable **ti** (rather than **te**).

Raising $\hat{7}$

This alteration of scale-degree $\hat{7}$ is extremely common in music that uses the minor scale.

Raising scale-degree $\hat{7}$ creates a relatively large gap of three semitones between scale-degrees $\hat{6}$ and $\hat{7}$. To smooth this out, composers sometimes raise scale-degree $\hat{6}$ as well. When scale-degree $\hat{6}$ is raised, it is still called a submediant, but is sung with the syllable *la* (rather than *le*). Note that $\hat{6}$ is rarely raised alone, but typically only in conjunction with raised $\hat{7}$.

Raising $\hat{6}$

By shifting the position of scale-degrees $\hat{7}$ or $\hat{6}$ and $\hat{7}$, we create new forms of the minor scale. The natural minor, the basic form of the scale, has $\hat{6}$ and $\hat{7}$ in their natural, unaltered position. When $\hat{7}$ is raised, the resulting scale is called **har-** *Harmonic minor* **monic minor.** When both $\hat{6}$ and $\hat{7}$ are raised, the resulting scale is called **ascending** *Asending melodic* **melodic minor.** Lesson 20 discusses these additional forms of the minor scale. *minor* *(↳ then LOWERED* *6th & 7th on the* *way down)*

Raising scale-degrees $\hat{7}$ or $\hat{6}$ and $\hat{7}$ from their natural position in the minor scale changes the dynamic qualities of the scale degrees. Now there is a flow of energy upward from scale-degree $\hat{5}$ to scale-degree $\hat{8}$, and the leading tone truly leads upward to the tonic.

Dynamic qualities

Lesson 17: In-class activities

1. **Singing.** Sing these three-note melodic fragments using scale-degree numbers, solfège syllables, or a neutral syllable like "la," as indicated by your instructor.

2. **Singing.** Sing these melodies using scale-degree numbers, solfège syllables, or a neutral syllable like "la," as indicated by your instructor.

3. **Singing.** Sing these melodies using scale-degree numbers, solfège syllables, or a neutral syllable like "la," as indicated by your instructor.

   a. Haydn, String Quartet (measures 1–4 and 5–8 begin the same but end differently).

Handwritten margin notes:

finding the key from key signature:
- for a major, it's the 2nd last ♭!
  Is though, piece is in G minor! (relative minor of B♭ major - scale deg. 6)

to make harmonic (6 minor) raise the 7th deg of scale

melodic minor
- 6th & 7th raised → up
- 6th & 7th lowered → down

b. Mozart, Sonata (adapted; as in the previous passage, measures 1–4 and 5–8 begin the same but end differently).

4. **Singing (improvise).** Continue and conclude the following short melodies (each should last four measures). Use only the notes of the A minor scale. Sing using scale-degree numbers, solfège syllables, or a neutral syllable like "la," as indicated by your instructor. You may perform your improvisation in continuing succession with other students, in tempo and without missing a beat. As one student concludes an improvisation, another begins immediately, starting with the two given measures and concluding with his or her own two-measure improvisation.

5. **Singing (improvise).** You are given a melody in whole notes. Using only the notes of A minor (including the possibility of raising scale-degrees $\hat{7}$ or $\hat{6}$ and $\hat{7}$), elaborate and decorate that melody. (See In-class activities 14-5, 15-4, and 16-4 for models.)

6. **Singing (duets).** Two students or groups of students sing the two lines of the following duets. Then switch parts. Sing using scale-degree numbers, solfège syllables, or a neutral syllable like "la," as indicated by your instructor.

7. **Dictation.** The instructor will play an A minor scale to establish a context and then will play a series of individual notes from the scale. Sing the note back with the correct scale-degree number or solfège syllable. The instructor will begin with A, C, and E only, then gradually add the remaining four notes.

8. **Dictation.** Within each group the instructor will play melodic patterns in a random order. Identify the pattern being played and then sing it back, either on a neutral syllable like "la" or using scale-degree numbers or solfège syllables.

9. **Playing.** Learn to play an A minor scale in one octave with your right hand alone and with your left hand alone (fingerings are provided). It is conventional to raise scale-degrees $\hat{6}$ and $\hat{7}$ when ascending and restore them to their natural position when descending.

10. **Playing.** Learn to play these melodies, sharing the playing between your left and right hands (fingerings are provided).

    a. Haydn, String Quartet

b. Mozart, Sonata (adapted)

11. Playing (improvise). In-class activities 17-4 and 17-5 involve improvisation. Instead of singing, perform your improvisations on the piano.

Name: _____

Date: _____

Instructor's Name: _____

LESSON 17: EXERCISES   *Important! Questions on the test*

17-1. Within the A minor scale, identify these notes with scale-degree numbers, scale-degree names, and solfège syllables, as indicated. (Both F and F♯ represent $\hat{6}$; both G and G♯ represent $\hat{7}$.)

a. scale-degree numbers

DO these

$\boxed{\hat{4}}$ $\hat{1}$ $\hat{5}$ $\hat{3}$ $\hat{1}$ $\hat{6}$ $\hat{2}$ $\hat{1}$

$\hat{2}$ $\hat{7}$ $\hat{3}$ $\hat{1}$ $\hat{6}$ $\hat{4}$ $\hat{2}$ $\hat{5}$

b. scale-degree names

$\boxed{\text{submediant}}$ tonic subdom. superton. dominant subtonic leading tone mediant

mediant leading tone subdom. tonic submed. dominant submed. subtonic

c. solfège syllables

$\boxed{do}$ ___ ___ ___ ___ ___ ___ ___

___ ___ ___ ___ ___ ___ ___ ___

17-2. Within the A minor scale, identify these notes with scale-degree numbers.

a. Haydn, String Quartet

b. Mozart, Sonata (adapted)

17-3. Compose a melody in A minor for each of these texts. If you wish, you may use the rhythms you previously composed for these texts in Exercise 9-5. Each melody is begun for you. Play your melodies on the piano or other instrument before handing them in—be sure they sound the way you want them to. Be prepared to sing your melodies in class.

a. O Captain! my Captain! our fearful trip is done. (Walt Whitman)

Name: _____

Date: _____

Instructor's Name: _____

b. Heard melodies are sweet, but those unheard
Are sweeter; therefore, ye soft pipes, play on.
(John Keats)

Heard mel - o - dies   are   sweet,

17-4. Fill in the blanks in these melodies by adding whatever notes from the A minor scale and whatever rhythmic values sound best to you. Bear in mind the dynamic tendencies of the different scale degrees. You may raise scale-degrees $\hat{6}$ and $\hat{7}$ when approaching the tonic from below. Play your melodies on the piano or other instrument before handing them in—be sure they sound the way you want them to. Be prepared to sing your melodies in class.

Lesson 18: Minor scales other than A minor

In this lesson you will learn about transposition, minor scales with sharps, minor scales with flats, and the circle of fifths.

Like major scales, minor scales are named for their tonic (scale-degree Î). The minor scale we have been considering so far has the note A as its tonic and is thus called an A minor scale. The A minor scale requires no accidentals, but **transposing** it to start on any other note will require flats or sharps to pre-serve its intervallic structure. To write the minor scale starting on E (the fifth degree of A minor), one sharp (F♯) is needed.

Transposition

E minor scale

G major

Without the F♯, there would be two steps of the wrong size: a semitone be-tween scale-degrees Î and 2̂ and a whole tone between scale-degrees 2̂ and 3̂. The F♯ makes all of the steps the correct size.

As with the major scale, every time we transpose up five steps in this way, an additional sharp is required.

A minor → major is wr, st

Minor scales with sharps

In contrast, to write a D minor scale, of which A is scale-degree $\hat{5}$, one flat (B♭) is needed.

D minor scale

Every time we transpose down five steps in this way, an additional flat is required.

Minor scales with flats

If we start on A and move up five steps at a time in one direction and down five steps at a time in the other, we will eventually meet back in the middle. We thus create a **circle of fifths** on which all of the minor scales and the accidentals needed to make them can be conveniently listed.

Circle of fifths

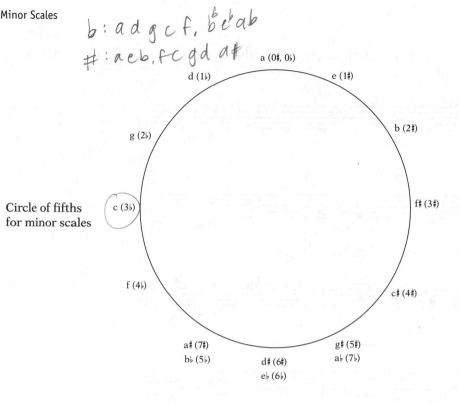

b: a d g c f, b♭e♭a♭ b
#: a e b, f c g d a#

Circle of fifths
for minor scales

Lesson 18: In-class activities

1. Singing. Sing the following common five-note patterns (given in B minor and G minor). Sing using scale-degree numbers, solfège syllables, or a neutral syllable such as "la," as directed by your instructor. Notice that these melodies routinely use an accidental (natural or sharp) to raise scale-degree $\hat{7}$, thus creating a leading tone.

2. Singing. Sing these melodies using scale-degree numbers, solfège syllables, or a neutral syllable such as "la," as directed by your instructor. Notice that these melodies routinely use an accidental (natural or sharp) to raise scale-degree $\hat{7}$ thus creating a leading tone.

a. Schubert, "Death and the Maiden" (D minor; the refusal of the melody to budge from D suggests Death's inexorability).

b. Chopin, Prelude in C minor (the melody descends a long way, mostly stepwise, to its conclusion on C4).

c. Bach, Fugue in G Major (although the piece begins and ends in G major, this passage is in E minor).

d. Bach, Fugue in G Major (although the piece begins and ends in G major, this passage is in B minor).

e. Bach, Fugue in G minor.

f. Bach, Fugue in G minor (although the piece begins and ends in G minor, this passage is in C minor).

g. Haydn, String Quartet (this passage is in A minor).

h. Haydn, String Quartet (despite the key signature, this passage is in D minor).

3. Singing (improvise). Continue and conclude the following short melodies (each should last four measures). Sing using scale-degree numbers, solfège syllables, or a neutral syllable like "la," as indicated by your instructor. You may perform your improvisation in continuing succession with other students, in tempo and without missing a beat. As one student concludes an improvisation, another begins immediately, starting with the two given measures and concluding with his or her own two-measure improvisation.

a.

b.

c.

4. Singing (improvise). You are given a melody in whole notes or half notes. Using only the notes of the appropriate minor key (including the possibility of raising scale-degrees $\hat{6}$ and/or $\hat{7}$), and whatever rhythmic values you like, elaborate and decorate that melody. See In-class activities 14-5, 15-4, and 16-4 for models.

a.

b.

c.

5. Singing (duets). Two students or groups of students sing the two lines of the following duets. Then switch parts. Sing using scale-degree numbers, solfège syllables, or a neutral syllable like "la," as indicated by your instructor.

6. Dictation. Within each group, the instructor will play the scales in a random order. One is minor, one is major, and one is neither. Identify the scale played.

7. Playing. You are given a note and told its scale degree. Play the appropriate minor scale down to its tonic, then up through an octave. When ascending, you may raise scale-degrees $\hat6$ and $\hat7$, as directed by your instructor.

8. Playing (improvise). You are given a note and told its scale degree. Starting with that note, improvise a short melody that ends on the tonic of the appropriate minor scale. When approaching the tonic from below, you should raise scale-degrees $\hat6$ and $\hat7$.

9. Playing. Learn to play minor scales with each hand alone and with both hands together. Here are five minor scales that have the same piano fingering.

(with $\hat{6}$ and $\hat{7}$ raised when ascending)

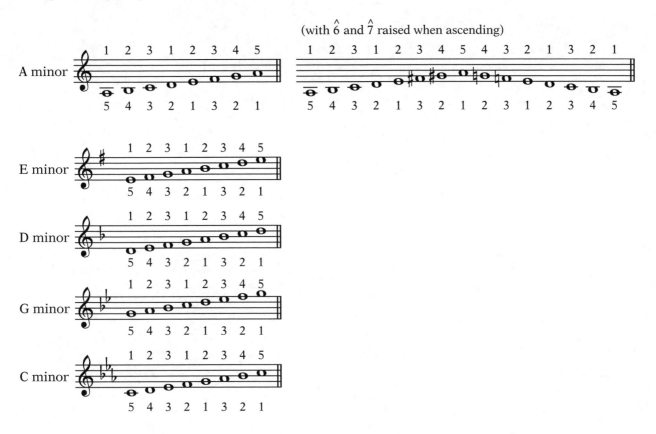

Name: _____

Date: _____

Instructor's Name: _____

LESSON 18: EXERCISES

circle of fifth is better to use (handwritten)

18-1. Write minor scales by adding the appropriate sharps or flats (minor scales with three or fewer accidentals).

mysearchlab

a. F# minor / C minor

b. G minor / A minor

c. E minor / G minor

d. D minor / B minor

18-2. Write minor scales by adding the appropriate sharps or flats (all minor scales).

mysearchlab

a. E minor / G# minor

b. D minor / F minor

c. Ab minor / D# minor

(handwritten margin notes:)
C = SD6 of Eb major
minor
toniz = 2nd last b
for b keys: toniz = 2nd last flat
- memorize the circle
c major & c minor =
toniz major/minors
can relate by
toniz note or
relative maj/minors

C → WT/ST = Eb   3b
Bb ≠ 2b
O
maj G(# 1)
2b
F 1b
D FC 2#

W TONE △ ST up
→ major key for
MINOR scale
eg. A min → C maj

G 1#
B 5# FCGDA
F 1b
G# → Ab maj = 4b
BEAD
Cb minor, 7b
F# 6#
FCGDAE

d. F# minor   A (3#)   G minor → B♭ → 2♭

e. A# minor   C#–7#   B minor →

f. B♭ minor   D♭ → 5♭   C# minor   E 4# FCGD

g. C minor   E♭ maj → 3♭   E♭ minor   G♭ → 6♭

BEADGC

18-3. You are given a note and told what scale degree it is. Write the appropriate minor scale (scales with three or fewer accidentals).

a. F# is $\hat{2}$ C is $\hat{7}$ D minor

E minor

b. D is $\hat{5}$ E♭   G minor   D is $\hat{4}$ A minor   ST WT

c. D is $\hat{6}$ F# minor   F# is $\hat{5}$ B minor

d. E♭ is $\hat{3}$ C minor   E is $\hat{2}$ D minor

ST at: 2–3,   5–6

Name: _____

Date: _____

Instructor's Name: _____

18-4. You are given a note and told what scale degree it is. Write the appropriate minor scale (all minor scales).

mysearchlab   **18-5.** You are given the name of a minor scale and a scale degree. Write the appropriate note (scales with three or fewer sharps or flats).

mysearchlab   **18-6.** You are given the name of a minor scale and a scale degree. Write the appropriate note (all minor scales).

Name: _____

Date: _____

Instructor's Name: _____

18-7. In these passages, identify the **major** or **minor** scales being used by writing them in the appropriate space beneath the score.

a. Bach, Fugue in G Major (the third scale is the same as the first).

b. Bach, Fugue in G minor (remember that scale-degree $\hat{7}$ is routinely raised in minor scales. Disregard the C♯ in parentheses in measure 5.)

Name: _____

Date: _____

Instructor's Name: _____

c. Schumann, Song (disregard the B♭ in parentheses in measure 5—it
   does not belong to the prevailing scale, but merely decorates the A,
   which does).

d. Mendelssohn, Piano Trio (here are three similar passages taken from three different places in the work. Disregard the notes in parentheses—they merely decorate notes that belong to the prevailing scales).

Name: _____

Date: _____

Instructor's Name: _____

18-8. Transpose these melodies as requested. When you transpose a melody, you start on a different note and proceed in a different key, but maintain the shape, internal structure (including all semitones and whole tones), and sound of the original. Transposition from one key to another always requires the use of accidentals (sharps or flats). Play your work on a piano or other instrument before handing it in—be sure it sounds the way you want it to.

to G minor

3

mysearchlab **18-9.** Compose a melody for each of these texts. The first is in E minor and the second is in G minor. If you wish, you may use the rhythms you previously composed for these texts in Exercise 10-4. Each melody is begun for you. Play your melodies on the piano or other instrument before handing them in—be sure they sound the way you want them to. Be prepared to sing your melodies in class.

a. Made weak by time and fate, but strong in will
To strive, to seek, to find, and not to yield.
(Alfred, Lord Tennyson)

Made   weak   by   time   and   fate,

b. Since then, at an uncertain hour,
That agony returns:
And till my ghastly tale is told,
This heart within me burns.
(Samuel Taylor Coleridge)

Since   then,   at   an   un - cer - tain hour,   That

Name: _____

Date: _____

Instructor's Name: _____

18-10. Fill in the blanks in these melodies by adding whatever notes from the appropriate minor scale and whatever rhythmic values sound best to you. Bear in mind the dynamic tendencies of the different scale degrees. You may raise scale-degrees $\hat{6}$ and $\hat{7}$ when approaching the tonic from below. Play your melodies on the piano or other instrument before handing them in—be sure they sound the way you want them to. Be prepared to sing your melodies in class.

Lesson 19: Minor keys and key signatures

In this lesson you will learn about minor keys, minor key signatures, relative keys, and parallel keys.

As with the major scale, each minor scale embodies a network of relationships, with its own unique tonic, supertonic, mediant, and so on. This network of relationships is what defines a **key.** A piece is in the key of D minor, for example, if it begins and ends by using the notes of the D minor scale and treats D as tonic, F as mediant, A as dominant, and so on. Every minor scale contains one and only one statement of each of the seven letter names (A, B, C, D, E, F, G)—only the accidentals vary, but this variety is enough to distinguish the scales from each other.

Key

Scale-degree Name Syllable	$\hat{1}$ tonic *do*	$\hat{2}$ supertonic *re*	$\hat{3}$ mediant *me*	$\hat{4}$ subdominant *fa*	$\hat{5}$ dominant *sol*	$\hat{6}$ submediant *le*	$\hat{7}$ subtonic *te*
A minor	A	B	C	D	E	F	G
E minor	E	F♯	G	A	B	C	D
B minor	B	C♯	D	E	F♯	G	A
F♯ minor	F♯	G♯	A	B	C♯	D	E
C♯ minor	C♯	D♯	E	F♯	G♯	A	B
G♯ minor	G♯	A♯	B	C♯	D♯	E	F♯
A♭ minor	A♭	B♭	C♭	D♭	E♭	F♭	G♭
D♯ minor	D♯	E♯	F♯	G♯	A♯	B	C♯
E♭ minor	E♭	F	G♭	A♭	B♭	C♭	D♭
A♯ minor	A♯	B♯	C♯	D♯	E♯	F♯	G♯
B♭ minor	B♭	C	D♭	E♭	F	G♭	A♭
F minor	F	G	A♭	B♭	C	D♭	E♭
C minor	C	D	E♭	F	G	A♭	B♭
G minor	G	A	B♭	C	D	E♭	F
D minor	D	E	F	G	A	B♭	C

Key signature
Circle of fifths

As with the major scale, the accidentals needed for each minor scale can be gathered into a **key signature,** and the key signatures for all of the minor scales can be summarized in a **circle of fifths.** The sharps and flats are added (and written) in just the same order as in major.

Minor key
signatures

Relative keys

Major and minor scales that share the same key signature are called **relative keys.** Relative keys use the same notes, but they are ordered differently. For example, F major and D minor both use the same seven notes, but F major arranges those notes to begin on F and D minor arranges them to begin on D. Similarly, D major and B minor are relative scales.

Relative scales

Major scales begin on scale-degree $\hat{3}$ of their relative minors; minor scales begin on scale-degree $\hat{6}$ of their relative majors.

The relative major and minor key signatures can be gathered into a double circle of fifths, with the major keys listed around the outside in uppercase letters, the minor keys around the inside in lowercase letters, and their shared key signatures between.

Relative keys

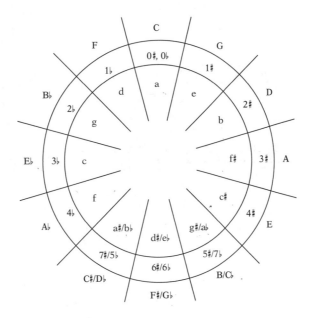

Major and minor scales that share the same tonic are called **parallel keys.** Parallel keys share not only the same tonic but also the same supertonic, subdominant, and dominant as well. C major and C minor, B♭ major and B♭ minor, D major and D minor are all parallel keys. They differ only in scale-degrees $\hat{3}$, $\hat{6}$, and $\hat{7}$. But those differences can have a powerful expressive effect. Many compositions create a change of mood by shifting from minor to major, or vice versa, while retaining the same tonic.

Parallel keys

Lesson 19: In-class activities

1. Singing. Sing the following common seven-note patterns (given in E minor and D minor). Sing using scale-degree numbers, solfège syllables, or a neutral syllable such as "la," as directed by your instructor.

2. Singing. Sing these melodies using scale-degree numbers, solfège syllables, or a neutral syllable such as "la," as directed by your instructor.

a. Rodríguez, "La Cumparsita" (adapted; the melody leaps from a low G to a high G, then fills in by step the space thus opened).

b. Chopin, Prelude in C minor (adapted; the generally descending shape of the melody contributes to its gloomy character).

c. Schubert, "Death and the Maiden" (the upward push of the melody reflects a young woman's desire to evade death).

d. Ellington, "It Don't Mean a Thing" (adapted; the melody stays between scale-degrees 1̂ and 5̂).

3. **Singing (improvise).** Continue and conclude the following short melodies (each should last four measures). Use only the notes of the appropriate minor scale. Sing using scale-degree numbers, solfège syllables, or a neutral syllable like "la," as indicated by your instructor. You may perform your improvisation in continuing succession with other students, in tempo and without missing a beat. As one student concludes an improvisation, another begins immediately, beginning with the two given measures and concluding with his or her own two-measure improvisation.

4. **Singing (improvise).** You are given a melody in dotted half notes. Using only the notes of the appropriate minor key (including the possibility of raising scale-degrees 6̂ and/or 7̂), and whatever rhythmic values you like, elaborate and decorate that melody. See In-class activities 14-5, 15-4, and 16-4 for models.

5. Singing (duets). Two students or groups of students sing the two lines of the following duets. Then switch parts. Sing using scale-degree numbers, solfège syllables, or a neutral syllable like "la," as indicated by your instructor.

6. Playing (improvise). You are given a key signature and a note. Starting with that note, improvise a short melody that ends on the tonic of the appropriate minor key.

7. Playing. Learn to play the following five-finger pattern in all minor keys. Play first with each hand alone and then with both hands together.

etc.

etc.

8. Playing. Learn to play the following five-finger pattern as it moves through all of the minor keys. The last note of each pattern becomes the first note of the next. Alternate hands.

etc.

Name: _____

Date: _____

Instructor's Name: _____

LESSON 19: EXERCISES

19-1. Identify the minor key represented by these key signatures (keys with three or fewer flats or sharps in the key signature).

19-2. Identify the minor key represented by these key signatures (all keys).

19-3. Write the key signature for these minor keys (keys with three or fewer sharps or flats in the key signature). Be sure to write sharps or flats in the correct order and position on the staff (see the circle of fifths diagram on p. 204 for models).

Name: _____

Date: _____

Instructor's Name: _____

19-4. Write the key signature for these minor keys (all keys). Be sure to write sharps or flats in the correct order and position on the staff (see the circle of fifths diagram on p. 204 for models).

mysearchlab 19-5. Name the key of these pieces. Remember that scale-degree $\hat{7}$ is routinely raised in minor keys.

a. Chopin, Prelude (notice that both staves are written in bass clef).

Key: _____

b. Schubert, "Death and the Maiden" (notice that both staves are written in bass clef).

Key: _____

c. Rodríguez, "La Cumparsita" (disregard the C♯ in measures 2 and 4—it does not belong to the scale, but embellishes the D, which does).

Key: _____

Name: _____

Date: _____

Instructor's Name: _____

d. Mozart, Sonata (disregard the embellishing notes in parentheses).

Key: _____

e. Ellington, "It Don't Mean a Thing" (the D♭ in measure 3 is a wonder-
fully expressive note, but it does not belong to the key—that's part
of the reason it sounds so expressive).

Key: _____

f. Haydn, String Quartet.

Key: _____

g. Bach, Fugue.

*Important as well!!

Key: _____

mysearchlab   **19-6.** Name the two keys (one major and one minor) represented by these key signatures (keys with three or fewer sharps or flats in the key signature). Write the major key first with an uppercase letter, then the minor key with a lowercase letter.

mysearchlab   **19-7.** Name the two keys (one major and one minor) represented by these key signatures (all keys). Write the major key first with an uppercase letter, then the minor key with a lowercase letter.

Name: _____

Date: _____

Instructor's Name: _____

19-8. For each minor key, name the relative major and provide their shared key signature (keys with three or fewer sharps or flats in the key signature). Remember to write the sharps and flats in the prescribed order and position.

19-9. For each minor key, name the relative major and provide their shared key signature (all keys). Remember to write the sharps and flats in the prescribed order and position.

mysearchlab   19-10. Compose a melody for each of these texts. If you wish, you may use the rhythms you previously composed for these texts in Exercise 11-4. Each melody is begun for you. Play your melodies on the piano or other instrument before handing them in—be sure they sound the way you want them to. Be prepared to sing your melodies in class.

a. What passing-bells for these who die as cattle?
   Only the monstrous anger of the guns.
   (Wilfred Owen)

b. And what rough beast, its hour come round at last,
   Slouches toward Bethlehem to be born?
   (W. B. Yeats)

Name: _____

Date: _____

Instructor's Name: _____

19-11. Fill in the blanks in these melodies by adding whatever notes from the appropriate minor scale and whatever rhythmic values sound best to you. Bear in mind the dynamic tendencies of the different scale degrees. You may raise scale-degrees $\hat{6}$ and $\hat{7}$ when approaching the tonic from below. Play your melodies on the piano or other instrument before handing them in—be sure they sound the way you want them to. Be prepared to sing your melodies in class.

Lesson 20: Harmonic and melodic minor

In this lesson you will learn about the harmonic minor and melodic minor scales.

The minor scale we have been discussing so far is called the **natural minor.** The natural minor is the basic form of the minor scale, and key signatures are always based on it. But as we observed in Lesson 17, scale-degrees $\hat{6}$ and $\hat{7}$ are frequently raised one semitone above their position in the natural minor. These alterations create new, varied forms of the minor scale.

Natural minor

The first common variant is the **harmonic minor.** It creates a leading tone by raising scale-degree $\hat{7}$ a semitone from its position in the natural minor.

Harmonic minor

Harmonic minor *↳ always raised 7th*

In the natural minor, scale-degree $\hat{7}$ is called the **subtonic** and is a whole step below the tonic. In the harmonic minor, scale-degree $\hat{7}$ is called the **leading tone** and is only a semitone below the tonic. It is as though the leading tone has been borrowed from the parallel major.

Subtonic → *natural minor*
Leading tone — *raised 7th. ST below only*

In the harmonic minor, there are three semitones: between scale-degrees $\hat{2}$–$\hat{3}$ and $\hat{5}$–$\hat{6}$ (as in the natural minor) and $\hat{7}$–$\hat{8}$ (borrowed from the parallel major). There is also a gap between scale-degrees $\hat{6}$–$\hat{7}$. This interval, a semitone larger than a whole tone, is called an **augmented second** (for reasons to be explained in Chapter 4).

Augmented second

Harmonic minor

To create the harmonic minor by raising scale-degree $\hat{7}$ from its position in the natural minor, an accidental will always be required. If scale-degree $\hat{7}$ in the natural minor is flat, it must be made natural; if scale-degree $\hat{7}$ in the natural minor is natural, it must be made sharp; if scale-degree $\hat{7}$ in the natural minor is sharp, it must be made double sharp.

A second common variant is the **melodic minor,** which exists in two forms: **ascending** and **descending.** In its ascending form, the melodic minor creates a leading tone by raising scale-degree $\hat{7}$ a semitone from its position in the natural minor, just as the harmonic minor does. It then smoothes out the gap between scale-degrees $\hat{6}$–$\hat{7}$ by also raising scale-degree $\hat{6}$ by a semitone. This variant is thus particularly suitable for singing or playing a melody that ascends to the tonic.

Ascending melodic minor

to get rid of augmented second

Ascending melodic minor

Now there are two semitones, between scale-degrees $\hat{2}$–$\hat{3}$ and $\hat{7}$–$\hat{8}$. All the other steps in the scale are whole tones. The ascending melodic is thus very similar to the major, differing only in the placement of one of its semitones—between $\hat{2}$ and $\hat{3}$ in minor and between $\hat{3}$ and $\hat{4}$ in major.

Ascending melodic

Major

To write an ascending melodic minor scale, scale-degrees $\hat{6}$ and $\hat{7}$ will always require an accidental.

Descending melodic minor

The final variant of the minor scale is called the **descending melodic minor.** When descending melodically from the tonic, the raised seventh degree (leading tone) and sixth degree are no longer necessary and revert to their positions in the natural minor. As a result, the descending form of the melodic minor is identical to the natural minor and thus requires no further discussion.

The three forms of the minor scale—natural, harmonic, and melodic—are not really three independent scales. Rather, the natural minor is the basic form of the minor scale, and the key signature is always based on it. Harmonic and melodic minor are just variants that result from the alteration of scale-degrees $\hat{7}$ or $\hat{6}$ and $\hat{7}$.

Lesson 20: In-class activities

The in-class activities for Lessons 17, 18, and 19 virtually all include alteration of scale-degrees $\hat{7}$ or $\hat{6}$ and $\hat{7}$ in minor and thus involve the harmonic and melodic minor scales. No new activities are provided here.

Name: _____

Date: _____

Instructor's Name: _____

LESSON 20: EXERCISES

20-1. Transform these natural minor scales into harmonic (H) or the ascending form of the melodic minor (MA) by adding or altering accidentals (minor scales with three or fewer sharps or flats in the key signature).

20-2. Transform these natural minor scales into harmonic (H) or the ascending form of the melodic minor (MA) by adding or altering accidentals (all minor scales). Hint: You will need a double sharp to raise scale-degree $\hat{7}$ for some of the minor keys whose tonic note is itself sharp.

F# minor (H) G minor (H)

A# minor (MA) F minor (H)

Bb minor (MA) C# minor (MA)

G# minor (H) Eb minor (H)

20-3. You are given a note and told that it is scale-degree $\hat{6}$ or $\hat{7}$ in either the harmonic minor (H) or ascending form of the melodic minor scale (MA). Write the scale (minor scales with three or fewer sharps or flats in the key signature).

a. F# is $\hat{7}$ (MA) C# is $\hat{7}$ (H)

b. D# is $\hat{7}$ (MA) D# is $\hat{6}$ (MA)

c. E is $\hat{6}$ (MA) F# is $\hat{6}$ (MA)

d. A# is $\hat{7}$ (H) A is $\hat{6}$ (MA)

Name: _____

Date: _____

Instructor's Name: _____

20-4. You are given a note and told that it is scale-degree $\hat{6}$ or $\hat{7}$ in either the harmonic minor (H) or the ascending form of the melodic minor scale (MA). Write the scale (all minor scales). Hint: You will need a double sharp to raise scale-degree $\hat{7}$ for some of the minor keys when the tonic note is itself sharp.

20-5. You are given the name of a minor scale and a scale-degree number. Write the appropriate note (scales with three or fewer sharps or flats in the key signature).

mysearchlab   20-6. You are given the name of a minor scale and a scale-degree number. Write the appropriate note (all minor scales).

Chapter 3: Supplementary Lesson   *[handwritten: ✕ on test]*

[handwritten: Alto clef + triplets review?]

In this lesson you will learn about the modes and the pentatonic scale.

[handwritten: 4. know how to name notes written on Alto clef.]

The major and minor scales are the most common scales in Western classical tonal music. Six additional scales were in common use in Medieval and Renaissance music (before around 1600). These are called the **modes,** or **Church modes,** and they persist in more recent folk and popular music. They can be played using only the white notes of the piano.

[handwritten: Modes ✕ find middle C, then count the lines]

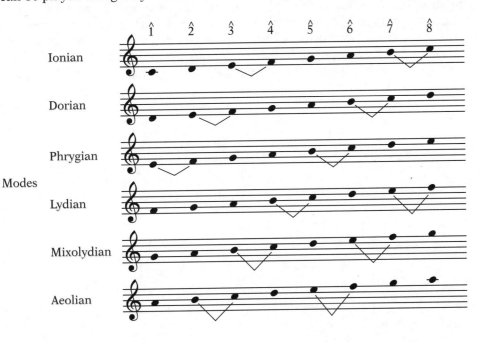

The six modes, like all other scales, may be transposed to start on any note. Notice the distinctive position of the two semitones in each mode and the way in which modal scales and key signatures relate to major and minor scales and key signatures.

Mode name	In relation to major and minor scales	Position of semitones	Key signature
Ionian	Same as major	3̂–4̂, 7̂–8̂	Normal for major
Dorian	Natural minor with raised sixth degree	2̂–3̂, 6̂–7̂	One sharp more (or one flat less) than signature for minor
Phrygian	Natural minor with lowered second degree	1̂–2̂, 5̂–6̂	One flat more (or one sharp less) than signature for minor
Lydian	Major with raised fourth degree	4̂–5̂, 7̂–8̂	One sharp more (or one flat less) than signature for major
Mixolydian	Major with lowered seventh degree	3̂–4̂, 6̂–7̂	One flat more (or one sharp less) than signature for major
Aeolian	Same as minor	2̂–3̂, 5̂–6̂	Normal for minor

Pentatonic scale

One final scale in reasonably common use, particularly in folk and popular music, is the **pentatonic scale,** so called because it contains five notes: a group of three and a group of two.

Pentatonic scale

It can be thought of as a major scale with scale-degrees $\hat{4}$ and $\hat{7}$ omitted (it thus contains no semitones). The notes can also be rearranged to give the feeling of Dorian, Phrygian, or minor (if the scale started on D, E, or A). Whatever its ordering, the pentatonic scale, like all other scales, can be transposed to start on any of the twelve notes. In one of its transpositions, the pentatonic scale corresponds to the black keys of the piano, with their grouping of three-plus-two or two-plus-three keys.

Chapter 3: Self-Test

1. Write scales as indicated (ascending within one octave). Use appropriate accidentals (do not use key signatures).

G major *F#*   F minor (natural)   *Ab maj = 4b*   *BEAD*

B minor (ascending melodic) *2# raise 6 & 7*   E major   *FC GD*

Ab major *4b*   D minor (harmonic) *F# (1b)*

2. You are given the name of a major or minor scale and a scale-degree number. Write the appropriate note.

F major: $\hat{4}$ G minor: $\hat{6}$ A minor: $\hat{7}$ (harmonic)   Ab major: $\hat{5}$ Eb major: $\hat{3}$ B minor: $\hat{4}$

E minor: $\hat{7}$ (ascending melodic)   Bb major: $\hat{6}$ D major: $\hat{2}$ E major: $\hat{4}$ C# minor: $\hat{5}$ F minor: $\hat{3}$

3. Write key signatures for these keys.

A major   D minor   E major   D major   F# minor   Eb minor

G minor   Bb major   E minor   Ab major   F major   C minor

4. Name the two keys, one major and one minor, represented by these key signatures.

Chapter 3: Self-Test (answer key)

1. Write scales as indicated (ascending within one octave). Use appropriate accidentals (do not use key signatures).

2. You are given the name of a major or minor scale and a scale-degree number. Write the appropriate note.

3. Write key signatures for these keys.

4. Name the two keys, one major and one minor, represented by these key signatures.

4 Intervals

Lesson 21: Interval size

In this lesson you will learn about intervals, melodic and harmonic intervals, interval size, and compound intervals.

An **interval** is the distance between two notes. When the two notes occur at the same time, the interval is **harmonic**. When one note occurs before the other, the interval between them is **melodic**, and may be either ascending or descending.

Intervals
Harmonic intervals
Melodic intervals

(handwritten: ⭒ Analyze SIZE first!! ↳ accidentals change quality not size)

(handwritten: 'SIZE = how its written   Quality = how many STs)

Harmonic intervals

Melodic intervals

Intervals are identified by both their **size** (to be discussed in this lesson) and their **quality** (to be discussed in the next lesson). The size of an interval is the number of steps it contains (or the number of different letter names it spans), **disregarding any accidentals**. A **unison** contains a single step: its two notes have the same letter name and lie on the same line or in the same space of the staff.

Interval size

Unison *(handwritten: Augmented unison – F → F# (unison b/c same letter name))*

(handwritten: # of ST tells you quality)

Unisons

A **second** contains two steps and consists of notes with adjacent letter names. The actual number of semitones between the notes may vary, but if one note is on a space and the other is on the adjacent line (or vice versa), the interval is a second. We have previously referred to this interval as a **step**.

Second *(handwritten box: major second = wt / minor seconds = ST)*

(handwritten: size first b4 semitones   F → G# = same # of semitones   F → Ab also 3 ST   ⭒ Y tells you quality.   ⭒ written on PAPER = tells you the size)

Seconds

(handwritten: Augmented 2nd = made higher   Diminished 2nd = made lower (can be same note but how its written))

231

[handwritten: can stack them : successive thirds]

Third   A **third** contains three steps and spans three letter names. As with seconds, the actual number of semitones may vary, but if the two notes are on adjacent lines or adjacent spaces, the interval is a third.

Fourth
Fifth
Sixth
Seventh
Octave

The remaining intervals—**fourths**, **fifths**, **sixths**, **sevenths**, and **octaves**— are calculated in the same way.

Simple intervals
Compound intervals

Intervals smaller than an octave are called **simple**. Intervals larger than an octave are **compound**, because they consist of a simple interval plus one or more octaves. Compound intervals are referred to either by their simple names or by the total number of steps they contain.

[handwritten: Compound 3rd (major 10) → red to 3rd]

[handwritten: reduction - easier to understand]
[handwritten: glorified 3rd → over an octave]

Fourth

Fifth

Sixth

Seventh

Lesson 21: In-class activities

Reciting. There are only seven letter-pairs for each interval size. Drill and memorize those pairs as follows.

a. Seconds. The letter-pairs for seconds are C–D, D–E, E–F, F–G, G–A, A–B, and B–C. Your instructor will name a note. Provide the note a second above or below, as requested.

b. Thirds. The letter-pairs for thirds are C–E, D–F, E–G, F–A, G–B, A–C, and B–D. Your instructor will name a note. Provide the note a third above or below, as requested.

c. Fourths. The letter-pairs for fourths are C–F, D–G, E–A, F–B, G–C, A–D, and B–E. Your instructor will name a note. Provide the note a fourth above or below, as requested.

d. Fifths. The letter-pairs for fifths are C–G, D–A, E–B, F–C, G–D, A–E, and B–F. Your instructor will name a note. Provide the note a fifth above or below, as requested.

e. Sixths. The letter-pairs for sixths are C–A, D–B, E–C, F–D, G–E, A–F, and B–G. Your instructor will name a note. Provide the note a sixth above or below, as requested.

f. Sevenths. The letter-pairs for sevenths are C–B, D–C, E–D, F–E, G–F, A–G, and B–A. Your instructor will name a note. Provide the note a seventh above or below, as requested.

Name: _____

Date: _____

Instructor's Name: _____

LESSON 21: EXERCISES

count only!. regardless of accidentals

21-1. Identify the numerical size of these simple intervals. Remember to disregard any accidentals—they do not affect the numerical size of an interval (1 = unison, 2 = second, 3 = third, 4 = fourth, 5 = fifth, 6 = sixth, 7 = seventh, 8 = octave).

mysearchlab

21-2. Identify the numerical size of these compound intervals. Remember to disregard any accidentals—they do not affect the numerical size of an interval. Compound seconds and thirds should be identified as ninths and tenths. Larger intervals should be identified as their simple equivalents (1 = unison, 2 = second, 3 = third, 4 = fourth, 5 = fifth, 6 = sixth, 7 = seventh, 8 = octave, 9 = ninth, 10 = tenth).

mysearchlab

21-3. Write intervals of the proper size as indicated. Remember to disregard any accidentals—they do not affect the numerical size of an interval.

Name: _____

Date: _____

Instructor's Name: _____

21-4. Identify the numerical size of these intervals. Remember to disregard any accidentals—they do not affect the numerical size of an interval.

a. Arlen, "Over the Rainbow" (each measure contains a leap down from B♭, and the leaps get bigger each time).

b. Chopin, Prelude in C minor (this bass line features wide leaps, mostly fourths and fifths).

c. Schubert, "Heidenröslein" (all of these intervals, between bass and melody, are compound—identify them as their simple equivalents [i.e., with a number smaller than 8]).

Lesson 22: Seconds and thirds

In this lesson you will learn about interval quality, natural intervals, major and minor intervals, diminished and augmented intervals, and enharmonically equivalent intervals.

Intervals of the same numerical **size** may vary in **quality** depending on the number of semitones they contain. If a second contains only one semitone, it is a **minor second** (familiar already as a semitone or a half step). If a second contains two semitones, it is a **major second** (familiar already as a whole tone or whole step). A **natural interval** is formed without any accidentals. There are seven **natural seconds**, all either major or minor.

Interval quality

Minor second
Major second
Natural intervals

Natural seconds

M   M   m   M   M   M   m

m → M → A
ST ST
larger larger

If both notes of a natural second are raised or lowered by the same amount, the size and quality of the interval remain the same.

Natural seconds transposed

If a minor second, or any minor interval, is compressed by lowering the upper note or raising the bottom note by a semitone, it becomes **diminished**. But diminished seconds—intervals made up of adjacent letter names that are enharmonically the same pitch—are rare and we will not consider them further here. If a major second, or any major interval, is expanded by lowering the bottom note or raising the upper note by a semitone, it becomes **augmented**.

Augmented second

Major, minor, and
augumented seconds

Major third
Minor third
Like seconds, thirds can be **diminished**, **minor**, **major**, or **augmented**. The seven **natural thirds**, formed without any accidental, are all either major (contain four semitones or two whole tones) or minor (contain three semitones or one whole tone and one semitone).

Natural thirds

Raising or lowering both notes by the same amount preserves the size and quality of the interval.

Natural thirds transposed

Natural thirds transposed (cont.)

When a minor third is compressed by a semitone, it becomes **diminished**; when a major third is expanded by a semitone, it becomes **augmented**. But these are relatively rare in music and will not concern us further here; instead, we will concentrate on major and minor thirds.

Major and minor thirds

In sum, there are four kinds of seconds and thirds (diminished, minor, major, and augmented), but only minor, major, and augmented seconds and minor and major thirds are in common use.

	Diminished	Minor	Major	Augmented
Seconds (number of semitones)	C♯–D♭ / 0	C–D♭ / 1	C–D / 2	C–D♯ / 3
Thirds (number of semitones)	C♯–E♭ / 2	C–E♭ / 3	C–E / 4	C–E♯ / 5

Enharmonic intervals

Intervals that span the same number of semitones but are spelled with different note names are **enharmonically equivalent**. C–D♯ and C–E♭, for example, both span three semitones, but one is a second and the other is a third. They have correspondingly different musical roles to play.

Enharmonically equivalent intervals

Augmented second   Minor third
(3 semitones)   (3 semitones)

Lesson 22: In-class activities

1. **Singing.** Sing the following melodies. The lyrics identify the qualities of the natural seconds and thirds.

a.

Ma-jor sec-ond, ma-jor sec-ond, mi-nor sec-ond, ma-jor sec-ond, ma-jor

sec-ond, ma-jor sec-ond, mi-nor sec-ond. Mi-nor sec-ond, ma-jor sec-ond, ma-jor

sec-ond, ma-jor sec-ond, mi-nor sec-ond, ma-jor sec-ond, ma-jor sec-ond.

b.

Ma-jor third, mi-nor third, mi-nor third, ma-jor third, ma-jor third, mi-nor third,

mi-nor third, yes!   Mi-nor third, ma-jor third,   ma-jor third, mi-nor third,

mi-nor third, ma-jor third,   mi-nor third, yes!

2. Dictation. The instructor will play the pairs of notes within each group
in a random order. Sing the notes you hear, then identify the interval as
a minor second, major second, minor third, major third, or none of the
above. In Groups 1–6, the three intervals are m2, M2, or neither of these;
in Groups 7–12, the three intervals are m3, M3, or neither of these.

3. Playing. Play the following melody two times. The first time, identify
the qualities of the thirds as you play them. The second time, identify the
qualities of the seconds as you play them. Transpose to other major keys.

Name: _____

Date: _____

Instructor's Name: _____

P4, P5, P8 = different rules

M3, m6, m7 maj & minor

= today!

LESSON 22: EXERCISES

22-1. Identify the quality of these natural seconds (m = minor, M = major).   **mysearchlab**

22-2. Identify the quality of these seconds (m = minor, M = major, A = augmented).   **mysearchlab**

22-3. Add an accidental (sharp or flat) to the top note if needed to create seconds of the desired quality (m = minor, M = major, A = augmented). Do not alter the bottom note.

22-4. Write seconds as indicated (m = minor, M = major, A = augmented).

Name: _____

Date: _____

Instructor's Name: _____

22-5. Identify the quality of these natural thirds (m = minor, M = major).

22-6. Identify the quality of these thirds (m = minor, M = major).

22-7. Add an accidental (sharp or flat) to the top note if needed to create thirds of the desired quality (m = minor, M = major). Do not alter the bottom note.

22-8. Write thirds as indicated (m = minor, M = major).

Name: _____

Date: _____

Instructor's Name: _____

22-9. Identify these intervals as seconds (minor, major, augmented) or thirds (major, minor).

    a. Haydn, String Quartet (thirds, ascending and descending, are a persistent feature of this melody).

    b. Schubert, "Death and the Maiden" (the first two seconds go down, the next two go up. Don't forget to take the key signature into account).

    c. Bach, Chorale (the voice pairs—soprano-alto, alto-tenor, and tenor-bass—are often very close to each other, either a third or a second apart. Don't forget to take the key signature into account).

Lesson 23: Sixths and sevenths

In this lesson you will learn about sixths and sevenths, enharmonically equivalent intervals, and interval inversion.

Sixths and sevenths behave like seconds and thirds. Natural sixths and sevenths are either major or minor (a **minor sixth** contains eight semitones, a **major sixth** contains nine semitones, a **minor seventh** contains ten semitones, and a **major seventh** contains eleven semitones).

Minor sixth
Major sixth
Minor seventh
Major seventh

When a natural sixth or seventh is transposed up or down, it retains the same quality.

When minor sixths and sevenths are compressed by a semitone, they become diminished; when major sixths and sevenths are expanded, they become

Augmented sixths

Diminished sevenths

augmented. Augmented sevenths and diminished sixths occur rarely and will not concern us further. **Augmented sixths** are somewhat more common (there is a beautiful example of one in measure 6 of Chopin's Prelude in C minor), but not enough to merit discussion and drill in an introductory textbook like this one. **Diminished sevenths** are also reasonably common.

Major and minor sixths   Major, minor, and diminished sevenths

Thus, while there are four kinds of sixths and sevenths (diminished, minor, major, and augmented) only major and minor sixths and major, minor, and diminished sevenths will be discussed here.

	Diminished	Minor	Major	Augmented
Sixths (number of semitones)	C#–A♭ / 7	C–A♭ / 8	C–A / 9	C–A# / 10
Sevenths (number of semitones)	C#–B♭ / 9	C–B♭ / 10	C–B / 11	C–B# / 12

As noted earlier, intervals that span the same number of semitones but are spelled with different note names are **enharmonically equivalent**. C♯–A♯ and C♯–B♭, for example, both span nine semitones, but one is a sixth and the other is a seventh.

Enharmonically equivalent intervals

Major sixth
(9 semitones)   Diminished seventh
(9 semitones)

When an octave is divided into two parts, each part is said to be the **inversion** of the other. Conversely, an interval can be combined with its inversion to make up an octave.

Interval inversion

Interval + inversion = Octave

Dividing an octave

An interval is **inverted** by reversing its upper and lower notes (bottom becomes top and top becomes bottom). To invert an interval, either move the upper note down an octave or move the lower note up an octave.

Inverting intervals

When an interval is inverted, certain predictable things happen to the size and quality. In size, seconds become sevenths (and vice versa) and thirds become sixths (and vice versa).

Inverting intervals (size)   **Second** ← inverts to → **Seventh**
Third ← inverts to → **Sixth**

In quality, major intervals become minor (and vice versa) and diminished intervals become augmented (and vice versa).

Inverting intervals (quality)   **Minor** ← inverts to → **Major**
Diminished ← inverts to → **Augmented**

For the seconds, thirds, sixths, and sevenths, the inversions work like this:

	d2	m2	M2	A2	d3	m3	M3	A3
Inverting intervals	↕	↕	↕	↕	↕	↕	↕	↕
	A7	M7	m7	d7	A6	M6	m6	d6

Lesson 23: In-class activities

1. **Singing.** Sing the following melody. The lyrics identify the qualities of the natural sixths.

Ma-jor sixth, ma-jor sixth,   mi-nor sixth, ma-jor sixth,   ma-jor sixth, mi-nor sixth,   mi-nor sixth, yes!

2. **Singing.** Sing the following melodies. Identify the qualities of the sixths and sevenths.

   a. Arlen, "Over the Rainbow" (this melody features large upward leaps).

   b. Haydn, String Quartet (the downward leaps that lead from beat 3 to beat 1 get larger and larger).

   c. Bach, Fugue in G minor (from the highest note to the lowest note of the melody is a diminished seventh).

   d. Bach, Fugue in G Major (this melody features two large upward leaps).

   e. Joplin, "The Entertainer" (this melody begins by repeating the sixth from E4 to C5, then explores the inversion of that interval: the third from C5 to E5).

f. Mendelssohn, Trio (the two halves of this melody begin with an upward leap and then fill in that space with descending steps).

3. Dictation. The instructor will play the pairs of notes within each group in a random order. Sing the notes you hear, then identify the interval as a minor sixth, major sixth, minor seventh, major seventh, or none of the above. In Groups 1–6, the three intervals are m6, M6, or neither of these; in Groups 7–12, the three intervals are m7, M7, or neither of these.

4. Playing. Play the following melody two times. The first time, identify the qualities of the sevenths as you play them. The second time, identify the qualities of the sixths as you play them. Transpose to other major keys.

Name: _____

Date: _____

Instructor's Name: _____

LESSON 23: EXERCISES

23-1. Identify the quality of these natural sixths (m = minor, M = major).

23-2. Identify the quality of these sixths (m = minor, M = major).

23-3. Add an accidental (sharp or flat) to the top note if needed to create sixths of the desired quality (m = minor, M = major). Do not alter the bottom note.

23-4. Identify the quality of these sixths (m = minor, M = major). Then write the inversion and identify its quality.

Name: _____

Date: _____

Instructor's Name: _____

23-5. Write sixths as indicated (m = minor, M = major).

23-6. Identify the quality of these natural sevenths (m = minor, M = major).

my**lab**

23-7. Identify the quality of these sevenths (d = diminished, m = minor, M = major).

my**lab**

23-8. Add an accidental (sharp or flat) to the top note if needed to create sevenths of the desired quality (d = diminished, m = minor, M = major). Do not alter the bottom note.

Name: _____

Date: _____

Instructor's Name: _____

23-9. Identify the quality of these sevenths (d = diminished, m = minor, M = major). Then write the inversion and identify its quality.

23-10. Write sevenths as indicated (d = diminished, m = minor, M = major).

23-11. Identify these intervals as sixths (major or minor) or sevenths (diminished, minor, or major).

a. Arlen, "Over the Rainbow."

b. Bach, Fugue in G minor (the large leap at the beginning opens up a space that is gradually filled in).

c. Bach, Fugue in G Major (apart from the two big upward leaps, the melody moves almost entirely stepwise).

d. Mendelssohn, Trio (the large leap at the beginning of measure 1 is answered by one even larger at the beginning of measure 3).

e. Haydn, String Quartet (this melody is unusual in having more leaps than steps).

Lesson 24: Fourths and fifths, unisons and octaves

In this lesson you will learn about perfect intervals, fourths and fifths, unisons and octaves, interval inversion, and enharmonically equivalent intervals.

Because of the relative purity of their sound, unisons, fourths, fifths, and octaves are **perfect** intervals. Perfect intervals cannot be major or minor. They can only be **diminished** (if compressed by a semitone), **perfect,** or **augmented** (if expanded by a semitone). The seven natural fourths are all perfect, except for F–B, which is augmented.

Perfect intervals
Diminished intervals
Augmented intervals

Natural fourths

The **augmented fourth** is sometimes called the **tritone** because it spans three whole tones (it contains six semitones, or exactly one half of the twelve-semitone octave). **Perfect fourths,** in contrast, span two whole tones and a semitone (or five semitones).

Augmented fourth
Tritone
Perfect fourths

P4, P5, and P8 (octaves)

Transposing a natural fourth preserves its size and quality.

Inverted intervals always have to add up to 9.

Natural fourths transposed

If a perfect fourth is expanded by a semitone, it becomes augmented; if a perfect fourth is compressed by a semitone, it becomes diminished. Diminished fourths are rare, however, and we will concentrate only on perfect and augmented fourths here.

Perfect and augmented fourths

Inversion

Fourths **invert** to fifths. Perfect intervals invert to perfect intervals and (as with seconds, thirds, sixths, and sevenths) diminished intervals invert to augmented intervals, and vice versa.

Inverting fourths and fifths

Perfect 4th   ⟷   Perfect 5th

Augmented 4th ⟷   Diminished 5th

All the natural fifths are perfect except for B–F, which is diminished.

Natural fifths

A **perfect fifth** contains seven semitones (or three whole tones and a semitone); a diminished fifth contains six semitones (or two whole tones and two semitones).

Perfect fifth

Transposing a natural fifth preserves its size and quality.

Natural fifths transposed

If a perfect fifth is expanded by a semitone, it becomes augmented; if it is compressed by a semitone, it becomes diminished. Augmented fifths are rare, however, and we will be concerned here only with perfect and **diminished fifths**.

Diminished fifth

Perfect and diminished fifths

Perfect and
diminished fifths
(cont.)

In sum, while fourths and fifths may be diminished, perfect, or augmented, we will be concerned here only with perfect and augmented fourths and with diminished and perfect fifths.

	Diminished	Perfect	Augmented
Fourths (number of semitones)	C♯–F 4	C–F 5	C–F♯ 6
Fifths (number of semitones)	C♯–G 6	C–G 7	C–G♯ 8

Enharmonic intervals   A diminished fifth and an augmented fourth both contain six semitones. They are thus **enharmonically equivalent**. They are the same absolute size but span a different number of steps.

Diminished fifth
5 steps

Augmented fourth
4 steps

6 semitones

6 semitones

Unison   Two notes on the same pitch create a perfect **unison**.

Perfect unisons

If one of the notes is a semitone higher than the other, but still maintains the same letter name, then the interval is an **augmented unison** (there is no such thing as a diminished unison). Normally, we will just refer to such intervals as **chromatic semitones**.

Chromatic semitone

contrast to
minor 2nd's

Augmented unisons
(chromatic semitones)

The **octave** is like the unison. A perfect octave is a single note repeated   **Octave**
an octave higher or lower.

Perfect octaves

As with the other perfect intervals, compressing a perfect octave by a
semitone produces a diminished octave; expanding a perfect octave by a semitone produces an augmented octave. But diminished and augmented octaves
will not be discussed further here.

Lesson 24: In-class activities

1. Singing. Sing the following melodies. The lyrics identify the qualities of
   the natural fourths and fifths.

2. Singing. Sing the following melodies. Identify the qualities of the fourths
   and fifths.

   a. Arlen, "Over the Rainbow" (the downward leaps arrive on successively
      lower notes: G–F–E♭–D).

   b. Chopin, Prelude in C minor (this bass line moves mainly in fourths
      and fifths).

c. Lang, Song (the interval in measure 4 is given an expressive, yearning quality by the fermatas over both notes—they should be sustained as long as the singer thinks appropriate).

d. Schubert, "Death and the Maiden."

3. Dictation. The instructor will play the pairs of notes within each group in a random order. Sing the notes you hear, then identify the interval as a perfect fourth, perfect fifth, augmented fourth/diminished fifth (without distinction), or none of the above.

4. Playing. Play the following melody two times. The first time, identify the qualities of the fourths as you play them. The second time, identify the qualities of the fifths as you play them. Transpose to other major keys.

Name: _____

Date: _____

Instructor's Name: _____

LESSON 24: EXERCISES

24-1. Identify the quality of these natural fourths (P = perfect, A = augmented).   **mysearchlab**

24-2. Identify the quality of these fourths (P = perfect, A = augmented).   **mysearchlab**

mysearchlab **24-3.** Add an accidental (sharp or flat) to the top note if needed to create fourths of the desired quality (P = perfect, A = augmented). Do not alter the bottom note.

mysearchlab **24-4.** Write fourths as indicated (P = perfect, A = augmented).

mysearchlab **24-5.** Identify the quality of these natural fifths (d = diminished, P = perfect).

Name: _____

Date: _____

Instructor's Name: _____

24-6. Identify the quality of these fifths (d = diminished, P = perfect).

24-7. Add an accidental (sharp or flat) to the top note if needed to create fifths of the desired quality (d = diminished, P = perfect). Do not alter the bottom note.

24-8. Write fifths as indicated (d = diminished, P = perfect).

24-9. You are given a fourth or a fifth. Identify its quality (d = diminished, P = perfect, A = augmented). Then write its inversion and identify its quality.

Name: _____

Date: _____

Instructor's Name: _____

24-10. Identify these intervals as fourths (perfect or augmented) or fifths (diminished or perfect).

   a. Arlen, "Over the Rainbow."

   b. Chopin, Prelude in C minor.

   c. Lang, Song.

   d. Schubert, "Death and the Maiden" (the melody consists mainly of two large downward leaps, and then two large intervals filled in by steps, also descending).

Lesson 25: Intervals in a major key

In this lesson you will learn about intervals in a major key, intervals in relation to scale degrees, and consonance and dissonance.

Within a **major** scale, the intervals formed between the tonic and the other scale degrees are all **major** or **perfect**: major second, major third, perfect fourth, perfect fifth, major sixth, and major seventh.

Major scale intervals

use prof's techniques!

Intervals in relation to the tonic

It is also interesting to think about the intervals that can be formed with all of the degrees of a major scale, not just the tonic. The most common interval in the major scale is the perfect fourth (or, if the interval is inverted, the perfect fifth)—there are six of them.

Six perfect fourths

Indeed, the entire major scale can be described as a chain of perfect fourths or perfect fifths. (You read the fifths going clockwise and the fourths going counterclockwise.)

Circle of fourths/fifths

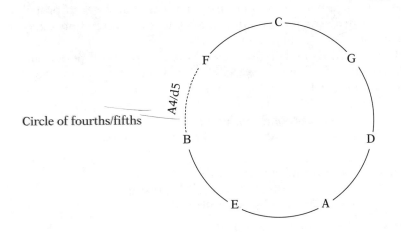

In addition to its six perfect fourths (or fifths), the major scale contains five major seconds (or minor sevenths), four minor thirds (or major sixths), three major thirds (or minor sixths), two minor seconds (or major sevenths), and a single, unique augmented fourth (or diminished fifth).

Other intervals

Five major seconds

Four minor thirds

Three major thirds

Two minor seconds

One augmented fourth

Every kind of interval occurs a different number of times, ranging from a maximum of six (perfect fourths/fifths) to a minimum of one (augmented fourth/diminished fifth). Because there is only one of them, the augmented fourth/diminished fifth plays an important key-defining role: it uniquely identifies the major scale to which it belongs. For example, the augmented fourth F–B and its inversion, the diminished fifth B–F, occur only in C major. Enharmonically equivalent intervals like F–C♭ and E♯–B point with equal force to other major keys (G♭ major and F♯ major).

Consonance
Dissonance

Harmonic intervals are classified as either **consonant** or **dissonant**. Consonant intervals are those that sound relatively harmonious, whose notes blend well together, and which are relatively stable. Composers use consonant intervals at points of arrival or conclusion. Dissonant intervals are those that sound relatively tense and unstable, with the notes rubbing against each other rather than blending together. Composers use dissonant intervals to propel music forward, because dissonances require some kind of continuation—they cannot be used at points of arrival or conclusion.

Major and minor thirds and sixths are consonant. So are all perfect intervals, with one partial exception: the perfect fourth, which is only consonant when a major or minor third or perfect fifth is sounding below it. When the lower note of the perfect fourth is also the lowest sounding note, the perfect fourth is usually treated as a dissonance. Major and minor seconds and sevenths are dissonant, as are all augmented and diminished intervals.

Consonance	**Major and minor thirds and sixths**
	Perfect fifths, octaves, and unisons
	Perfect fourths (sometimes)
Dissonance	**Seconds and sevenths**
	Augmented or diminished intervals
	Perfect fourths (sometimes)

Lesson 25: In-class activities

1. **Singing.** Sing the following melody using scale-degree numbers, solfège syllables, or a neutral syllable such as "la," as directed by your instructor.

2. **Singing (duets).** Sing one or more to a part, and then switch parts. Identify the melodic intervals (within each part) and the harmonic intervals (between the parts).

   a. In this duet the intervals between the parts are all consonances.

   b. In this duet the intervals between the parts are all consonances.

   c. Bach, Chorale (these are the soprano and bass voices in the first phrase of the chorale).

d. Bach, Chorale (these are the soprano and bass voices in the last phrase of the chorale).

e. Haydn, String Quartet (after singing this duet, listen to measures 2–5 of the piece from which it was adapted. Many pieces can be understood as elaborations of a simple, consonant duet like this one).

f. Mozart, "Dove sono" (after singing this duet, listen to the first eight measures of the piece from which it was adapted).

g. Mozart, Sonata (after singing this duet, listen to the first eight measures of the piece from which it was adapted).

3. Dictation. The instructor will play the three brief duets in a random order within each group. Identify the duet and sing it back.

4. Playing. Practice major scales in thirds and fifths. These can be played with either hand alone or with both hands together. The example is given in D major and also should be transposed to other major keys.

5. Playing. You are given an interval that occurs in more than one major key. Improvise a short progression of intervals that leads to the tonic note of one of the possible keys played in unison or an octave apart. Use only thirds, fifths, and sixths (in addition to the concluding unison or octave).

6. Playing. You are given an augmented fourth (which represents scale-degrees $\hat{4}$ and $\hat{7}$ in one key) and its enharmonic interval, a diminished fifth (which represents scale-degrees $\hat{7}$ and $\hat{4}$ in a different key). Play the resolution of each interval to scale-degrees and in the appropriate key.

Name: _____

Date: _____

Instructor's Name: _____

LESSON 25: EXERCISES

25-1. For the given keys, identify the requested intervals.

   a. G major: its four minor thirds <u>A–C, B–D, E–G, F♯–A</u>

   b. G major: its three major thirds _____

   c. F major: its five major seconds _____

   d. D major: its two minor seconds _____

   e. B♭ major: its one augmented fourth _____

   f. A major: its six perfect fourths _____

   g. E♭ major: its four minor thirds _____

25-2. For any major key, identify the interval between these scale degrees, always calculating upward from the first note to the second.

   a. $\hat{1}$–$\hat{5}$ <u>P5</u>

   b. $\hat{1}$–$\hat{3}$ _____

   c. $\hat{1}$–$\hat{6}$ _____

   d. $\hat{1}$–$\hat{7}$ _____

   e. $\hat{4}$–$\hat{6}$ _____

   f. $\hat{5}$–$\hat{7}$ _____

   g. $\hat{3}$–$\hat{4}$ _____

   h. $\hat{4}$–$\hat{7}$ _____

   i. $\hat{7}$–$\hat{4}$ _____

   j. $\hat{5}$–$\hat{6}$ _____

   k. $\hat{5}$–$\hat{1}$ _____

   l. $\hat{5}$–$\hat{2}$ _____

   m. $\hat{7}$–$\hat{5}$ _____

   n. $\hat{2}$–$\hat{6}$ _____

   o. $\hat{2}$–$\hat{7}$ _____

   p. $\hat{6}$–$\hat{1}$ _____

25-3. Name the major scales that contain these intervals.

a. F–A= $\hat{1}$–$\hat{3}$ in F, $\hat{4}$–$\hat{6}$ in C, $\hat{5}$–$\hat{7}$ in B♭

b. G–B = $\hat{1}$–$\hat{3}$ in _____ , $\hat{4}$–$\hat{6}$ in _____ , $\hat{5}$–$\hat{7}$ in _____

c. E–F= $\hat{3}$–$\hat{4}$ in _____ , $\hat{7}$–$\hat{8}$ in _____

d. D–A= $\hat{1}$–$\hat{5}$ in _____ , $\hat{2}$–$\hat{6}$ in _____ , $\hat{3}$–$\hat{7}$ in _____ ,
   $\hat{4}$–$\hat{1}$ in _____ , $\hat{5}$–$\hat{2}$ in _____ , $\hat{6}$–$\hat{3}$ in _____

e. F♯–A= $\hat{2}$–$\hat{4}$ in _____ , $\hat{3}$–$\hat{5}$ in _____ , $\hat{6}$–$\hat{1}$ in _____ ,
   $\hat{7}$–$\hat{2}$ in _____

f. B♭–C= $\hat{1}$–$\hat{2}$ in _____ , $\hat{2}$–$\hat{3}$ in _____ , $\hat{4}$–$\hat{5}$ in _____ ,
   $\hat{5}$–$\hat{6}$ in _____ , $\hat{6}$–$\hat{7}$ in _____

g. B♭–E= $\hat{4}$–$\hat{7}$ in _____

h. G♯–D= $\hat{7}$–$\hat{4}$ in _____

i. A♭–D= $\hat{4}$–$\hat{7}$ in _____

j. C♯–G= $\hat{7}$–$\hat{4}$ in _____

k. A♭–E= $\hat{7}$–$\hat{4}$ in _____

25-4. Identify the quality and size of these intervals. (Remember that the key signature remains in force throughout each line of music.)

Name: _____

Date: _____

Instructor's Name: _____

25-5. Identify the quality and size of these intervals. (Remember that the key signature remains in force throughout each line of music.)

a. Bach, Chorale

1.	M3	5.	___	9.	___	13.	___	17.	___	21.	___
2.	___	6.	___	10.	___	14.	___	18.	___	22.	___
3.	___	7.	___	11.	___	15.	___	19.	___	23.	___
4.	___	8.	___	12.	___	16.	___	20.	___	24.	___

b. Mendelssohn, Piano Trio

1.	m3	4.	___	7.	___	10.	___	13.	___	16.	___
2.	___	5.	___	8.	___	11.	___	14.	___	17.	___
3.	___	6.	___	9.	___	12.	___	15.	___	18.	___

25-6. Compose duets by adding a melody above the given melody (some notes are already provided). Play your duet on the piano or other instrument before handing it in—be sure it sounds the way you want it to. Be prepared to sing in class both the melody you are given and the melody you have composed. Your melody should follow these guidelines:

1. Use only whole notes.

2. Create only the following intervals between the two melodies: thirds, fifths, sixths, octaves. Identify each interval by writing the appropriate number beneath the staff.

3. Do not write two consecutive fifths or octaves between the melodies.

4. Write a melody that moves mainly by step. Your melody should be as smooth, connected, and directed as the melodies you are given.

5. Do not use any accidentals (sharps or flats).

Lesson 26: Intervals in a minor key

In this lesson you will learn about intervals in a minor key and intervals in relation to scale degrees.

In a **minor** scale, all of the intervals formed with the tonic, with one exception, are **minor** or **perfect**: major second (that's the exception), minor third, perfect fourth, perfect fifth, minor sixth, and minor seventh.

Minor scale intervals

Intervals in relation to the tonic

In a major scale, the intervals formed with the third, sixth, and seventh scale degrees are all major; in a minor scale these intervals are all minor. And that is precisely what gives the two scales their different, contrasting characters.

Considering all of the intervals (not just those formed in relation to the tonic), the minor scale (like the major) has six perfect fourths/perfect fifths, five major seconds/minor sevenths, four minor thirds/major sixths, three major thirds/minor sixths, two minor seconds/major sevenths, and one augmented fourth/diminished fifth. But those intervals are formed by different scale degrees.

Six perfect fourths

Five major seconds

Four minor thirds

Three major thirds

Two minor seconds

One augmented fourth

Also like the major scale, the minor scale can be described as a chain of perfect fourths/perfect fifths.

Circle of fourth/fifths

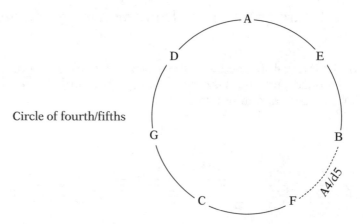

The alteration of scale-degrees $\hat{6}$ and $\hat{7}$ so common in minor, creates new intervals. The most important and distinctive of these is the augmented second (and its inversion, the diminished seventh) when $\hat{7}$ is raised to create a leading tone.

Augmented second/
diminished seventh

Like the augmented fourth/diminished fifth in major, this unique, distinctive interval involves the leading tone and thus serves to identify the tonic of the minor scale to which it belongs.

Lesson 26: In-class activities

1. **Singing.** Sing the following melody using scale-degree numbers, solfège syllables, or a neutral syllable such as "la," as directed by your instructor.

2. **Singing (duets).** Sing one or more to a part, and then switch parts. Identify the melodic intervals (within each part) and the harmonic intervals (between the parts).

a. In this duet, the intervals between the parts are all consonances.

b. In this duet, the intervals between the parts are all consonances.

c. Bach, Chorale (these are the soprano and bass voices).

d. Ellington, "It Don't Mean a Thing" (after singing this duet, listen to the passage from which it was adapted—see if you can figure out which one. Many pieces can be understood as elaborations of a simple, consonant duet like this one).

e. Chopin, Prelude in C minor, adapted (after singing this duet, listen to measures 5–8 of the piece from which it was adapted. The upper voice descends immediately from E♭ to C; the lower voice descends more slowly from C to E♭).

f. Schubert, "Death and the Maiden" (after singing this duet, listen to the first eight measures of the piece from which it was adapted).

3. Dictation. The instructor will play the three brief duets in a random order within each group. Identify the duet and sing it back.

4. Playing. Practice minor scales in thirds and fifths. These can be played with either hand alone or with both hands together. The example is given in D minor and also should be transposed to other minor keys.

5. Playing. You are given an interval that occurs in more than one minor key. Improvise a short progression of intervals that leads to the tonic note of one of the possible keys played in unison or an octave apart. Use only thirds, fifths, and sixths (in addition to the concluding unison or octave).

Example:

A minor   G minor   E minor   D minor

a.

b.

c.

d.

Name: _____

Date: _____

Instructor's Name: _____

LESSON 26: EXERCISES

26-1. For the given keys, identify the requested intervals.

> a. E minor: its three major thirds <u>G–B, C–E, D–F♯</u>

   b. E minor: its four minor thirds _____

   c. D minor: its six perfect fourths _____

   d. B minor: its three major thirds _____

   e. G minor: its one augmented fourth _____

   f. F♯ minor: its two minor seconds _____

   g. C minor: its five major seconds _____

26-2. For any minor key, identify the interval between these scale degrees, always calculating upward from the first note to the second.

> a. $\hat{1}$–$\hat{5}$ P5

   b. $\hat{1}$–$\hat{3}$ _____

   c. $\hat{1}$–$\hat{6}$ _____

   d. $\hat{1}$–$\hat{7}$ _____

   e. $\hat{1}$–♯$\hat{7}$ _____

   f. $\hat{4}$–$\hat{6}$ _____

   g. $\hat{5}$–$\hat{7}$ _____

   h. $\hat{5}$–♯$\hat{7}$ _____

   i. ♯$\hat{7}$–$\hat{4}$ _____

   j. $\hat{2}$–$\hat{6}$ _____

   k. ♯$\hat{7}$–$\hat{6}$ _____

   l. $\hat{6}$–♯$\hat{7}$ _____

   m. $\hat{5}$–$\hat{1}$ _____

   n. $\hat{5}$–$\hat{2}$ _____

   o. $\hat{5}$–$\hat{3}$ _____

   p. $\hat{6}$–$\hat{1}$ _____

26-3. Name the minor scales that contain these intervals.

> a. G–B = $\hat{3}$–$\hat{5}$ in <u>e</u>, $\hat{6}$–$\hat{8}$ in <u>b</u>, $\hat{7}$–$\hat{2}$ in <u>a</u>

   b. C–E = $\hat{3}$–$\hat{5}$ in _____, $\hat{6}$–$\hat{8}$ in _____, $\hat{7}$–$\hat{2}$ in _____

   c. B–C = $\hat{2}$–$\hat{3}$ in _____, $\hat{5}$–$\hat{6}$ in _____

   d. G–D = $\hat{1}$–$\hat{5}$ in _____, $\hat{3}$–$\hat{7}$ in _____, $\hat{4}$–$\hat{8}$ in _____, $\hat{5}$–$\hat{2}$ in _____, $\hat{6}$–$\hat{3}$ in _____, $\hat{7}$–$\hat{4}$ in _____

   e. G–B♭ = $\hat{1}$–$\hat{3}$ in _____, $\hat{2}$–$\hat{4}$ in _____, $\hat{4}$–$\hat{6}$ in _____, $\hat{5}$–$\hat{7}$ in _____

f. E–F♯ = 1̂–2̂ in _____, 3̂–4̂ in _____,
   4̂–5̂ in _____, 6̂–7̂ in _____, 7̂–8̂ in _____

g. E–B♭ = 2̂–6̂ in _____

h. G♯–D = 2̂–6̂ in _____

i. E♭–A = 6̂–2̂ in _____

26-4. Name the minor scales that contain the following augmented seconds
       (or diminished sevenths), when scale-degree 7̂ is raised.

a. B♭–C♯   D minor

b. D♯–C   _____

c. D–E♯   _____

d. A♭–B   _____

e. A♯–G   _____

f. F♯–E♭   _____

26-5. Identify these intervals.

Name: _____

Date: _____

Instructor's Name: _____

26-6. Identify the quality and size of these intervals. (Remember that the key signature remains in force throughout each line of music.)

a. Bach, Chorale.

1. M6	4. ___	7. ___	10. ___	13. ___	16. ___
2. ___	5. ___	8. ___	11. ___	14. ___	17. ___
3. ___	6. ___	9. ___	12. ___	15. ___	18. ___

b. Chopin, Prelude in C minor (adapted) (interval number twelve is an augmented sixth).

1. m6	4. ___	7. ___	10. ___	13. ___	16. ___	19. ___	22. ___
2. ___	5. ___	8. ___	11. ___	14. ___	17. ___	20. ___	23. ___
3. ___	6. ___	9. ___	12. A6	15. ___	18. ___	21. ___	24. ___

26-7. Compose duets by adding a melody above the given melody (some notes are already provided). Play your duet on the piano or other instrument before handing it in—be sure it sounds the way you want it to. Be prepared to sing in class both the melody you are given and the melody you have composed. Your melody should follow these guidelines:

a. Use only whole notes.

b. Create only the following intervals between the two melodies: thirds, fifths, sixths, octaves. Identify each interval by writing the appropriate number beneath the staff.

c. Do not write two consecutive fifths or octaves between the melodies.

d. Write a melody that moves mainly by step. Your melody should be as smooth, connected, and directed as the melodies you are given.

e. Do not use any accidentals (sharps or flats)—the leading tone in the penultimate measure is provided.

Chapter 4: Supplementary Lesson

In this lesson you will learn about all intervals, doubly diminished and doubly augmented intervals, and intervals in harmonic and melodic minor.

In the preceding lessons of Chapter 4, we focused on those intervals that occur most commonly. The following charts offer a more comprehensive account, identifying each interval by its size, quality, and the number of semitones it contains.

Seconds	Diminished second 0 semitones (C#–Db)	Minor second 1 semitone (C#–D)	Major second 2 semitones (C–D)	Augmented second 3 semitones (C–D#)
Thirds	Diminished third 2 semitones (C#–Eb)	Minor third 3 semitones (C–Eb)	Major third 4 semitones (C–E)	Augmented third 5 semitones (C–#)
Sixths	Diminished sixth 7 semitones (C#–Ab)	Minor sixth 8 semitones (C–Ab)	Major sixth 9 semitones (C–A)	Augmented sixth 10 semitones (C–A#)
Sevenths	Diminished seventh 9 semitones (C#–Bb)	Minor seventh 10 semitones (C–Bb)	Major seventh 11 semitones (C–B)	Augmented seventh 12 semitones (C–B#)

Unisons	Diminished unison (Does not exist—no interval can have fewer than 0 semitones)	Perfect unison 0 semitones (C–C)	Augmented unison 1 semitone (C–C#)
Fourths	Diminished fourth 4 semitones (C#–F)	Perfect fourth 5 semitones (C–F)	Augmented fourth 6 semitones (C–F#)
Fifths	Diminished fifth 6 semitones (C–Gb)	Perfect fifth 7 semitones (C–G)	Augmented fifth 8 semitones (C–G#)
Octaves	Diminished octave 11 semitones (C–Cb)	Perfect octave 12 semitones (C–C)	Augmented octave 13 semitones (C–C#)

consonant / dissonant

3rds & 6ths   2nd & 7ths

Dim 2nds, Aug 7ths

Doubly diminished
Doubly augmented

In fact, there are additional intervals not included on this chart. If you compress the size of a diminished interval it becomes **doubly diminished**. If you increase the size of an augmented interval, it becomes **doubly augmented**. Here are examples of doubly diminished and doubly augmented thirds and fifths.

But doubly diminished and doubly augmented intervals are so rare in music—there are no scales and few musical contexts that produce them—as to make any further discussion unnecessary.

The common procedure of raising scale-degree $\hat{7}$ in minor keys (creating a scale called the harmonic minor) produces intervals that are not available in the natural minor scale.

The intervals formed between scale-degrees $\hat{7}$ and $\hat{6}$ (diminished seventh/augmented second) and between scale-degrees $\hat{7}$ and $\hat{3}$ (diminished fourth/augmented fifth) cannot be found either in the major scale or in the unaltered minor scale.

Chapter 4: Self-Test

1. Identify these intervals by numerical size and quality (d = diminished, m = minor, M = major, P = perfect, A = augmented).

2. Write the requested interval above the given note.

| P5 | m3 | A4 | M2 | P4 | m6 | M3 |

| P8 | m7 | P5 | m3 | M7 | P4 | M6 |

3. Name all the keys, major and minor, that contain these intervals.

G–D   _____

C–E   _____

C♯–D   _____

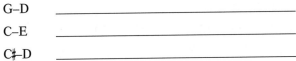

Chapter 4: Self-Test (answer key)

1. Identify these intervals by numerical size and quality (d = diminished, m = minor, M = major, A = augmented).

m3   P5   A4   M2   P8   m3   m6

P5   P4   m3   m7   m3   A4   m2

m6   m3   A4   M2   P8   m3   P4

2. Write the requested interval above the given note.

P5   m3   A4   M2   P4   m6   M3

P8   m7   P5   m3   M7   P4   M6

3. Name all the keys, major and minor, that contain these intervals.

   G–D   G, g, F, e, E♭, D, d, C, c, b, B♭, a

   C–E   C, a, G, F, e, d

   C♯–D   D, b, A, f♯

5 Triads and Seventh Chords

Lesson 27: Triads

In this lesson you will learn about triads (root, third, and fifth), triad qualities (major, minor, diminished, augmented), natural triads, and chord symbols.

The **triad** is the basic harmony of tonal music. It consists of three notes: a fifth divided into two thirds.

Triad

chords are named based on root

Triads   fifth ⟨ 𝄞 ⟩ third / third   fifth ⟨ 𝄞 ⟩ third / third

The three notes of a triad can always be written on three consecutive lines or three consecutive spaces. When they are written like that, the lowest note is called the **root**, the middle note is called the **third**, and the highest note is called the **fifth**. ⤷ *root position = on the bottom, stacked thirds.*

Root bottom
Third — middle
Fifth top   *spaced out on score*

open position vs. closed position (stacked 3rds)

Root, third, fifth   𝄞 fifth ← third ← root   𝄞 fifth ← third ← root

✱ ① Name chord.

There are four different qualities of triads—**major**, **minor**, **diminished**, and **augmented**—depending on the qualities of the thirds and fifths they contain. A **major triad** has a major third and a perfect fifth above the root (and thus a minor third between the two upper notes). A **minor triad** has a minor third and a perfect fifth above the root (and thus a major third between the two upper notes). The major and minor triads are sometimes called **consonant triads** or **perfect triads** because of their inherent stability. A **diminished triad** consists of a minor third and a diminished fifth above a root (or two consecutive minor thirds). An **augmented triad** consists of a major third and an augmented fifth (or two consecutive major thirds). *mark this down!*

Major triad

Minor triad

Diminished triad

Augmented triad

✱ ② = Quality of the chord · will have to name diff qualities of triads

Triad qualities — Major, Minor, Diminished, Augmented

Any note can act as the root of a triad. A triad is named for its root so, for example, a C♯ major triad is major in quality and has C♯ as its root, while an F minor triad is minor in quality and has F as its root. Here are some examples of major and minor triads:

· work from root pos. to change the triads

③ Inversions of chords

Major and minor triads

C♯ major   F minor   G minor   A major

Natural triads   There are seven **natural triads** (formed without any accidentals): C–E–G, D–F–A, E–G–B, F–A–C, G–B–D, A–C–E, and B–D–F. Of these, three are **major**, three **minor**, and one **diminished**.

Natural triads

The natural triads can also be visualized around a circle of thirds: each natural triad consists of three consecutive notes of the circle.

By applying accidentals to these seven natural triads, it is possible to form any triad. For example, we can build the four different kinds of triads that share E as their root by applying accidentals to G and B, the other two notes of the natural triad on E: E–G–B.

Forming triads

Conversely, every possible triad uses the groups of three letter names defined by the seven natural triads: C–E–G, D–F–A, E–G–B, F–A–C, G–B–D, A–C–E, and B–D–F.

Chord symbols   Composers and performers of jazz and popular music use a system of *not useful* **alphabetical chord symbols** to name triads and other chords. Major triads are named with a capital letter that designates the root of the triad. Minor triads are named with a capital letter followed by a lowercase m (for minor). Diminished triads are named by a capital letter followed either by a small circle or the abbreviation "dim." An augmented triad is named by a capital letter followed by a plus sign (+). These symbols are illustrated here with triads built on the root D.

Chord symbols

The augmented triad is included here only for the sake of theoretical completeness. In musical practice, it is rare and occurs only under special conditions. As a result, the augmented triad is not discussed further in this book, or included among the in-class activities or exercises.

So far, all of the triads discussed have been arranged in a tight little cluster, with the third and fifth found as close as possible above the root. But in actual music, many other arrangements are possible. One or more notes may be **doubled**, that is, represented by two or more different notes a unison or an octave apart. As a result, a three-note triad often appears in music as a chord containing four or more notes. Furthermore, the notes of a triad, including the notes that are doubled, may be **arpeggiated**, that is, with the notes played consecutively rather than simultaneously. Rhythmic and melodic activity can serve to animate and activate a triad.

Doubling

Arpeggiation

To figure out what triad is being played, eliminate all doublings and arrange the three notes in the smallest possible stack, on three adjacent lines or spaces. The lowest note in the stack is the root of the triad.

Identifying triads

G major   G minor

Lesson 27: In-class activities

1. Singing. With the given notes as root, arpeggiate major and minor triads up and down. Sing the names of the notes.

Example:

a.

b.

c.

d.

e.

2. Singing. You are given a note and told if it is the root, third, or fifth. Arpeggiate down to the root, then arpeggiate the major or minor triad up and down. Sing the names of the notes.

a.
b.
c.
d.

3. Singing (improvise). Choose a major or minor triad. Improvise a short melody that uses only the notes of that triad. Here are two samples:

4. Dictation. The instructor will play these three-note chords in a random order within each group. Identify each as a major triad, a minor triad, or not a triad.

5. Playing. Play the requested triads with either hand (use the fingering 1–3–5). Remember that major triads are named with a capital letter, minor triads with a lowercase m, and diminished triads with a ° sign.

a. Cm   play: C–E♭–G

b. G

c. Dm

d. Bm

e. E♭

f. F

g. A♭

h. F♯°

i. E

j. B°

k. A

l. D

m. Fm

n. G♯m

o. Gm

p. C♯m

q. Em

r. Am

s. D°

t. B♭

6. Playing. You are given a note; its identity as root, third, or fifth; and a triad quality. Play the triad.

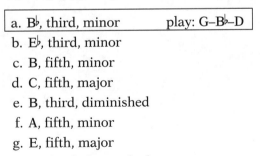

a. B♭, third, minor   play: G–B♭–D

b. E♭, third, minor

c. B, fifth, minor

d. C, fifth, major

e. B, third, diminished

f. A, fifth, minor

g. E, fifth, major

h. D, third, diminished

i. F♯, third, major

j. D, third, major

7. Playing. Play major and minor chords by changing the position of notes in the right hand while playing the root in the left hand.

a. D
b. Cm
c. Dm
d. E♭
e. Em
f. F
g. G
h. Gm
i. A
j. B♭

Name: _____

Date: _____

Instructor's Name: _____

LESSON 27: EXERCISES

27-1. Identify the qualities of these natural triads (M = major, m = minor, d = diminished).

27-2. Create the requested quality of triad by adding accidentals if needed to the third and/or fifth of these natural triads (M = major, m = minor, d = diminished). Do not alter the root.

27-3. Write triads as indicated. Remember that a capital letter alone calls for a major triad; a lowercase m calls for a minor triad; and ° calls for a diminished triad.

27-4. You are given a note as the root, third, or fifth of a certain quality of triad (M = major, m = minor, d = diminished). Add two more notes to complete the appropriate triad. Do not alter the note you are given.

27-5. Rewrite these triads in the closest possible position. Identify them with chord symbols (e.g., Em for E minor, G♯° for G♯ diminished, B♭ for B♭ major).

Name: _____

Date: _____

Instructor's Name: _____

27-6. Identify the boxed triads with chord symbols (e.g., Em for E minor, G#° for G# diminished, B♭ for B♭ major).

    a. Schumann, Song (the triads are formed by a combination of the voice and piano parts).

1. _____   2. _____   3. _____   4. _____   5. _____

b. Handy, "St. Louis Blues."

1. ____   2. ____   3. ____

c. Rodríguez, "La Cumparsita" (the notes in parentheses are embellishing or decorative—they do not belong to any triad. Do not include them in your identification of the triads).

1. ____   2. ____   3. ____   4. ____   5. ____

Name: _____

Date: _____

Instructor's Name: _____

d. Chopin, Prelude in C minor (notice that the upper piano notes are written in bass clef until near the end of the passage. The chords marked with an asterisk (*) have an additional fourth note a seventh above the root—ignore that note. On the third beat of each measure, the melody has a dissonant note that is excluded from the chord).

1. Cm	5. ____	9. ____	13. ____
2. ____	6. ____	10. ____	14. ____
3. ____	7. ____	11. ____	15. ____
4. ____	8. ____	12. ____	16. ____

root = ☐ nothing

Lesson 28: Triads in inversion

In this lesson you will learn about soprano and bass, inversion of triads (root position, first inversion, second inversion), and figured bass ($^5_3$, $^6_3$, $^6_4$).

The highest note in a chord is called the **soprano**; the lowest note is called the **bass**. When the root of the triad is in the bass (i.e., when the root of the triad is the lowest-sounding note), the triad is in **root position**. All the triads we have discussed thus far are in root position. But the third or fifth of the triad may also be in the bass. When that is the case, the triad has been **inverted**. When the third of the triad is in the bass, the triad is in **first inversion**. When the fifth of the triad is in the bass, it is in **second inversion**. Notice that the bass alone determines the position of the triad.

Soprano
Bass
Root position

First inversion
Second inversion

Triads in inversion

The first inversion of a triad is usually a weaker, less stable version of the root position. The second inversion, however, involves a significant difference. Recall that the interval of the perfect fourth is considered either consonant or dissonant, depending on the circumstances. In root position and first inversion, fourths occur among the upper voices and are thus consonant. In the second inversion, however, the fourth occurs between the bass and one of the upper voices—now there is nothing sounding below it and it is considered dissonant. As a result, a triad in second inversion is usually treated as a dissonant chord, and is used only under special circumstances, to be described later.

Fourths in triads

It is common to describe the position of triads, and other chords, using **figured bass** numbers. These numbers identify the intervals formed above a bass note (the lowest-sounding note). When a triad is in root position, there are intervals a fifth and a third above the bass, so the triad is said to be in $^5_3$ **position**.

Figured bass

$^5_3$ position

Triads in $^5_3$ position
(root position)

Notice that either or both the third and the fifth may be compound intervals and may be doubled. Notice also that the note creating a third with the bass may be either higher or lower than the note creating a fifth with the bass. The

[handwritten margin notes: root = nothing □ / 1st inversion = 6/3 / 2nd inversion = 6/4]

root may also appear doubled among the upper voices, an octave above the bass, but the number 8 is not normally included in the figured bass.

When a triad is in first inversion, there are intervals a sixth and a third above the bass, so the triad is said to be in $\frac{6}{3}$ **position**.

$\frac{6}{3}$ position

Triads in $\frac{6}{3}$ position (first inversion)

As with triads in $\frac{5}{3}$ position, the sixth and third may be doubled, may be compound, and may occur above or below each other.

$\frac{6}{4}$ position

A triad in second inversion is in $\frac{6}{4}$ **position**, with intervals a sixth and a fourth above the bass.

Triads in $\frac{6}{4}$ position (second inversion)

The sixth and the fourth may be compound and may occur above or below each other.

Chord symbols

Alphabetical **chord symbols** do not usually distinguish between the root position and inversions of a triad. Sometimes, however, composers indicate the position of a triad by providing the bass note following the chord symbol. The letter before the slash identifies the root of the triad and the letter after the slash identifies the actual bass note (which is the third or fifth of the triad).

[handwritten note: JAZZ - won't be doing these]

Chord symbols

Lesson 28: In-class activities

1. **Singing.** You are given a note as the bass note of a triad in first or second inversion. Arpeggiate upward through the rest of the triad. End an octave above where you began.

2. **Dictation.** The instructor will play these triads in a random order within each group. Identify them as root position ($\frac{5}{3}$), first inversion ($\frac{6}{3}$), or second inversion ($\frac{6}{4}$).

3. Playing. Play triads as indicated with either hand. (Remember that a capital letter stands for a major triad, a lowercase m for a minor triad, and ° for a diminished triad. In alphabetic chord symbols, the letter after the slash is the bass note.)

a. E_3^6 play: G♯–B–E

b. D_3^6

c. Fm_3^6

d. Cm_4^6

e. $E\flat_3^5$

f. A_3^6

g. $B\flat_3^6$

h. F_4^6

i. $F\sharp^{\circ}\,_3^6$

j. $E^{\circ}\,_3^6$

k. C_3^6

l. $A\flat_3^5$

m. $D\sharp^{\circ}\,_3^5$

n. Am_3^6

o. Fm/A♭   play: A♭–C–F

p. G♯°/B

q. Dm/A

r. Gm/B♭

s. F♯°/A

t. Cm/E♭

Name: _____

Date: _____

Instructor's Name: _____

LESSON 28: EXERCISES

28-1. You are given triads in root position (the figured bass is $\frac{5}{3}$). Rewrite them in first inversion (figured bass: $\frac{6}{3}$) and second inversion (figured bass: $\frac{6}{4}$).

28-2. Write triads as indicated. Remember that $\frac{5}{3}$ signifies root position, $\frac{6}{3}$ signifies first inversion, and $\frac{6}{4}$ signifies second inversion. In the alphabetic chord symbols, a capital letter stands for a major triad, a lowercase m for a minor triad, and ° for a diminished triad. If there is a letter after a slash, that is the bass note.

e.   Fm/A♭   B°/D   C/E   G♯°/B   Am/C   Dm/A

f.   Gm/B♭   D/F♯   F♯°/A   Em/G   A/E   Cm/E♭

28-3. You are given triads in first or second inversion. Rewrite them in root position. Remember that you can always write a triad in root position on three adjacent lines or spaces of the staff.

28-4. Identify the boxed triads by chord symbol (e.g., G for G major, Gm for G minor, and G° for G diminished) and figured bass numbers to indicate position ($\frac{5}{3}$ for root position, $\frac{6}{3}$ for first inversion, and $\frac{6}{4}$ for second inversion).

a. Mozart, "Dove sono" (chords 7, 13, 20, 22, and 26 are seventh chords—they contain an additional note a seventh above the root. Disregard this note. Chords 5, 11, and 12 contain only two notes—they are incomplete. Assume that the fifth of the triad has been omitted. Ignore the notes in parentheses—they function as decorative embellishments, not as members of any triad).

Name: _____

Date: _____

Instructor's Name: _____

1. __B♭⁵₃__   5. _____   9. _____   13. _____   17. _____   21. _____   25. _____

2. _____   6. _____   10. _____   14. _____   18. _____   22. _____   26. _____

3. _____   7. _____   11. _____   15. _____   19. _____   23. _____   27. _____

4. _____   8. _____   12. _____   16. _____   20. _____   24. _____

b. Bach, Chorale (ignore the decorative notes in parentheses. Chords 11 and 14 are incomplete—the fifth of the triad is omitted. Notice that in chord 8, the soprano is still singing its E—that note is part of both chords 7 and 8).

1. _____   4. _____   7. _____   10. _____   13. _____   16. _____   19. _____

2. _____   5. _____   8. _____   11. _____   14. _____   17. _____   20. _____

3. _____   6. _____   9. _____   12. _____   15. _____   18. _____   21. _____

c. Haydn, String Quartet (ignore the notes in parentheses).

1. _____   2. _____   3. _____   4. _____

d. Schubert, "Death and the Maiden" (notice that the upper staff of the piano part is in bass clef throughout).

Gib   dei - ne   Hand,   du   schön   und zart   Ge -   bild!
Give   me your   hand,   you   beau - ti - ful,   sweet   creature!

1. _____   2. _____   3. _____   4. _____

Lesson 29: Triads in major keys

In this lesson you will learn about triad names, Roman numerals, and triad qualities in major keys.

[handwritten: • analyzing via Roman numerals!]

A triad can be built on each degree of a major scale using the notes of that scale. (We will use C major as our example, but all of the relationships can be transposed to any other major scale.) The **name** of the triad is the name of its root: tonic, supertonic, mediant, subdominant, dominant, submediant, and leading tone.

Triad names

[handwritten: • or by scale degree analysis]

Triad names

Tonic   Supertonic   Mediant   Subdominant   Dominant   Submediant   Leading tone

Triads also can be named using **Roman numerals**, with the numerals corresponding to the scale degrees of the triad roots.

Roman numerals

Roman numerals

I   ii   iii   IV   V   vi   vii°

Of the seven triads in a major scale, three are major in **quality** (I, IV, and V), three are minor (ii, iii, and vi), and one is diminished (vii°). Note that for major triads, the Roman numeral is uppercase, for minor triads it is lowercase, and for diminished triads it is lowercase with a ° sign.

Triad qualities

Triad qualities

M   m   m   M   M   m   d

In identifying chords, Roman numerals are often combined with figured bass numbers: the Roman numeral identifies the root of the chord; the figured bass numbers tell the position of the chord.

Triads in major

C   Dm   Em   F   G   Am   B°

$I\frac{5}{3}$ $ii\frac{5}{3}$ $iii\frac{5}{3}$ $IV\frac{5}{3}$ $V\frac{5}{3}$ $vi\frac{5}{3}$ $vii°\frac{5}{3}$

[handwritten: root pos]

C/E   Dm/F   Em/G   F/A   G/B   Am/C   B°/D

$I\frac{6}{3}$ $ii\frac{6}{3}$ $iii\frac{6}{3}$ $IV\frac{6}{3}$ $V\frac{6}{3}$ $vi\frac{6}{3}$ $vii°\frac{6}{3}$

[handwritten: 1st inversion]

The figured bass $\frac{5}{3}$ is usually omitted—any Roman numeral without a figured bass after it will be assumed to be in root position ($\frac{5}{3}$ position). The figured bass $\frac{6}{3}$ is sometimes abbreviated 6 (the 3 is just assumed). In theory, it is also possible to construct $\frac{6}{4}$ chords on each degree of the scale. In musical practice, however, $\frac{6}{4}$ chords are used only under special conditions to be discussed in Chapter 6. Therefore, $\frac{6}{4}$ chords are omitted from the in-class activities and written exercises for this lesson. Another aspect of these harmonies, namely their functional relationships to each other and their combination into meaningful harmonic progressions, will also be deferred until Chapter 6.

Lesson 29: In-class activities

1. **Singing.** Sing the following arpeggiations of triads in a major key. Here are some ways to perform them: (1) sing on a neutral syllable like "la"; (2) sing with solfège syllables; (3) sing the qualities of the triads ("Ma-jor triad, mi-nor triad, mi-nor triad," etc.); (4) transpose to other major keys and sing the letter names of the notes.

2. **Dictation.** The instructor will play short progressions of triads in a random order within each group. Identify the progression you hear. Sing the bass.

Group 3

$$I \quad I^6 \quad V \qquad I \quad IV^6 \quad V \qquad I \quad IV \quad V$$

3. **Playing.** Play triads in C major as shown. Transpose to other major keys. In the first progression, all of the chords are in root position (they are $\frac{5}{3}$ chords). In the second progression, all of the chords are in first inversion (they are $\frac{6}{3}$ chords).

4. **Playing.** You are given a triad that could occur in several different major keys (each minor triad could be ii, iii, or vi; each major triad could be I, IV, or V). Beginning with that triad, play triads down to each of the possible tonics, then up through an octave.

Name: _____

Date: _____

Instructor's Name: _____

LESSON 29: EXERCISES

29-1. Use Roman numerals and figured bass numbers to identify these triads in major keys.

mysearchlab

29-2. You are given a major key and a Roman numeral with figured bass numbers. Write the appropriate triad.

a.

D: ii⁶   E♭: IV   G: V⁶   F: V   B♭: vii°⁶   A: I⁶

b.

A: V⁶   F: IV⁶   D: I⁶   B♭: I⁶   G: ii   E♭: vi

c.

B♭: ii⁶   G: vii°⁶   E♭: I⁶   F: ii   D: V   A: vi

d.

A: vii°⁶   B♭: V   G: IV   F: V⁶   E♭: V⁶   D: IV⁶

mysearchlab

29-3. Use Roman numerals and figured bass numbers to identify triads in these works.

a. Haydn, String Quartet (disregard the notes in parentheses—they are embellishing notes and do not belong to any triad. In this passage, there is one triad per measure. The passage begins and ends on the tonic).

C major: I

b. Bach, Chorale (disregard the notes in parentheses. This passage begins and ends on the tonic).

D major:

Name: _____

Date: _____

Instructor's Name: _____

c. Schumann, Song (this passage moves from tonic to dominant).

G major: _____

d. Mozart, "Dove sono" (there is generally one harmony per beat, consisting of a bass note plus a chord, except at the ends of the two
phrases—measure 8 and measures 17–18—where harmonies last
for a full measure. Disregard notes in parentheses—they embellish
the harmonies. In three places, there are chords we have not yet
studied and the Roman numerals are provided—these are inversions of the dominant seventh chord, V^7).

C major: ___

(continued)

Lesson 30: Triads in minor keys

In this lesson you will learn about triad names, Roman numerals, triad qualities in minor keys, and the effect of raising the leading tone.

As with the major, it is possible to build a triad on each degree of a minor scale. (We will use the key of A minor as our example, but all of the relationships can be transposed to other minor keys.) The **name** of each triad is the name of its root: tonic, supertonic, mediant, subdominant, dominant, submediant, and subtonic. Roman numerals also are used to name triads.

Triad names

Triad names

i	ii°	III	iv	v	VI	VII
Tonic	Supertonic	Mediant	Subdominant	Dominant	Submediant	Subtonic

In using the dominant and subtonic triads, composers routinely raise the seventh degree of the minor scale to create a leading tone (as discussed in Chapter 3). This gives these harmonies a greater impetus to move toward i (tonic). The common alteration in minor keys of scale-degrees $\hat{6}$ and $\hat{7}$ has the potential to affect other chords also, but use of a raised $\hat{7}$ to make V and vii° triads is by far the most common. As a result, the V and vii° chords are the same in major and minor keys.

Alternative forms of V and VII

v   altered to   V   VII   altered to   vii°
                        (subtonic)   (leading tone)

In the rest of this book, as in most music, we will assume that the dominant triad will be a major chord (V) and the leading-tone triad will be a diminished chord (vii°), both using the raised form of scale-degree $\hat{7}$. Of the seven triads in a minor scale, then, typically three are major in **quality** (III, V, and VI), two are minor (i and iv), and two are diminished (ii° and vii°).

Triad qualities

Triad qualities

m	d	M	m	M	M	d
i	ii°	III	iv	V	VI	vii°

In identifying chords, **Roman numerals** are combined with figured bass numbers. As in major keys, the figured bass numbers are usually omitted when the triad is in $\frac{5}{3}$ position and abbreviated to 6 when the triad is in $\frac{6}{3}$ position. Also as in major, $\frac{6}{4}$ chords occur relatively rarely and under special conditions to be discussed later. They are thus omitted here.

Roman numerals

Triads in minor

Lesson 30: In-class activities

1. **Singing.** Sing the following arpeggiations of triads in a minor key. Here are some ways to perform them: (1) sing on a neutral syllable like "la"; (2) sing with solfège syllables; (3) sing the qualities of the triads ("Mi-nor triad, di-min-ished triad, ma-jor triad," etc.); (4) transpose to other minor keys and sing the letter names of the notes. Notice that scale-degree $\hat{7}$ is routinely raised in minor in making the V and vii° chords.

2. Dictation. The instructor will play short progressions of triads in a random order within each group. Identify the progression you hear. Sing the bass.

Group 3

3. **Playing.** Play triads in the key of A minor as shown. Transpose to other major keys. Notice that scale-degree $\hat{7}$ is routinely raised for the V and vii° chords.

4. **Playing.** You are given a triad that could occur in several different minor keys (minor triads could be i or iv; major triads could be III, V, or VI). Beginning with that triad, play triads down to each of the possible tonics, then up through an octave. Be sure to raise the leading tone in the V and vii° chords.

Example:

= i in E minor   = iv in B minor

Name: _____

Date: _____

Instructor's Name: _____

LESSON 30: EXERCISES

30-1. Use Roman numerals and figured bass numbers to identify these triads in minor keys.

mysearch**lab**

30-2. You are given a minor key and a Roman numeral with figured bass numbers. Write the appropriate triad. Remember that scale-degree $\hat{7}$ is always raised in making the V and vii° chords.

a.

d: ii°6   f♯: VI   c: i6   b: III   g: V   e: vii°6

b.

e: ii°6   g: i6   d: vii°6   f♯: ii°6   C: III   b: V

c.

f♯: III   c: VI   b: iv   d: i6   e: V   g: iv6

d.

g: V6   e: VI   c: vii°6   f♯: vii°6   b: i6   d: iv

mysearch**lab**

30-3. Use Roman numerals and figured bass numbers to identify triads in these works.

a. Schubert, "Death and the Maiden" (when you see a chord that contains only two notes, assume that it is an incomplete triad with the fifth of the triad omitted. In this passage, the young woman ceases begging for her life and Death begins his unforgiving answer. Notice that the upper staff of the piano part is in bass clef starting in the middle of the third measure and disregard the notes in parentheses).

rüh - re mich nicht an.
do not touch me.

Der Tod. (Death)

Gib dei - ne Hand,   du schön und zart Ge - bild!   bin
Give me your hand,   you beau - ti - ful, sweet creature!

pp dim.   **pp**

D minor: i6

Name: _____

Date: _____

Instructor's Name: _____

    b. Bach, Chorale (disregard the notes in parentheses).

C minor: ___   ___   ___   _____   ___

Lesson 31: Seventh chords

In this lesson you will learn about seventh chords, major-minor (dominant) seventh chords, inversions of seventh chords, dominant seventh chords in major and minor keys, figured bass symbols, and chord names.

A **seventh chord** consists of a triad plus the interval of a seventh over a shared root. Or you can think of a seventh chord as a triad (a stack of two thirds) with an additional third on top of the stack. A seventh chord contains a **root**, **third**, **fifth**, and **seventh** and can be written on four successive lines or spaces on the staff.

Seventh chords

Seventh chords

Qualities

The quality of a seventh chord depends on the **qualities** of the triad and seventh that comprise it. The most important kind of seventh chord is called a **major-minor seventh chord**, because it consists of a **major triad** and a **minor seventh**. Or you can think of it as a major triad with a minor third added on top.

Major-minor seventh chord

Major-minor seventh chords

The major-minor seventh chord is also called a **dominant seventh chord**, because it is the quality you get when you build a seventh chord on the scale-degree $\hat{5}$ (the dominant) in a major key. As with triads, seventh chords can be named in two ways: (1) a Roman numeral that identifies the scale degree of the root; or (2) an alphabetical chord symbol, with the root identified by a letter.

Dominant seventh chord

Dominant seventh chords in major

In minor keys, scale-degree $\hat{7}$ is raised when creating a dominant seventh chord. As a result, a minor key and its parallel major will have the same dominant seventh chord.

Dominant seventh chords in minor

As with triads, seventh chords whose root is also the lowest-sounding note (bass) are said to be in **root position**. And, also as with triads, seventh chords can be **inverted** by placing notes other than the root in the bass: **First inversion** places the third of the seventh chord in the bass; **second inversion** places the fifth in the bass; **third inversion** places the seventh in the bass.

Root position
First inversion
Second inversion
Third inversion

Inversions of seventh chords

Figured bass
Chord symbols

Figured bass numbers are often used in conjunction with Roman numerals to indicate inversion. **Chord symbols** are also useful for indicating inversion: the actual bass note is shown after a slash.

not used

Figured bass and chord symbols

Lesson 31: In-class activities

1. Singing. With the given notes as root, arpeggiate major-minor seventh chords (dominant seventh chords) up and down. Sing on a neutral syllable such as "la" or with the names of the notes. Name the two keys (a major key and its parallel minor) of which this chord would function as V⁷.

2. Dictation. The instructor will play short progressions of chords in a random order within each group. Each progression contains a dominant seventh chord or one of its inversions ($\frac{6}{5}$ = first inversion; $\frac{4}{3}$ = second inversion; $\frac{4}{2}$ = third inversion). Identify the progression you hear. Sing the bass.

Group 1

$$\text{V}^7 \qquad \text{V}^6_5 \qquad \text{V}^4_3 \qquad \text{V}^4_2$$

Group 2

$$\text{V}^7 \qquad \text{V}^6_5 \qquad \text{V}^4_3 \qquad \text{V}^4_2$$

3. Playing. Play the requested major-minor seventh chord with either hand. Remember that $\frac{6}{5}$ = first inversion; $\frac{4}{3}$ = second inversion; and $\frac{4}{2}$ = third inversion. In the alphabetic chord symbols, the letter after the slash is the bass note.

a. E^7 play: E–G♯–B–D	k. E$^6_5$
b. A^7	l. D$^4_3$
c. G^7	m. B$^4_3$
d. B^7	n. F$^4_3$
e. C^7	o. E$^4_2$
f. D^7	p. A$^4_2$
g. F^7	q. B♭^{7}/D
h. B♭$^6_5$	r. D^7/F♯
i. C$^6_5$	s. C^7/B♭
j. A$^6_5$	t. B^7/F♯

4. Playing. You are given eight V⁷ chords. Resolve each to the root and third of its tonic triad (which may be either major or minor).

Name: _____

Date: _____

Instructor's Name: _____

LESSON 31: EXERCISES

31-1. Create major-minor (dominant) seventh chords by adding accidentals (if needed) to the upper three notes. Do not alter the lowest note. Remember that a major-minor seventh chord has a major triad and a minor seventh above its root.

31-2. Write major-minor (dominant) seventh chords as indicated (root position only). Remember that a major-minor seventh chord has a major triad and a minor seventh above its root.

31-3. You are given a note as the root, third, fifth, or seventh of a major-minor (dominant) seventh chord. Write the rest of the chord in root position. Do not alter the note you are given.

31-4. You are given major-minor (dominant) seventh chords in root position. Rewrite them in first inversion (the third of the chord is in the bass), second inversion (the fifth of the chord is in the bass), and third inversion (the seventh of the chord is in the bass).

a.

D^7 D^6_5 D^4_3 D^4_2 C^7 C^6_5 C^4_3 C^4_2

b.

$B\flat^7$ $B\flat^6_5$ $B\flat^4_3$ $B\flat^4_2$ $E\flat^7$ $E\flat^6_5$ $E\flat^4_3$ $E\flat^4_2$

c.

G^7 G^6_5 G^4_3 G^4_2 F^7 F^6_5 F^4_3 F^4_2

31-5. Write major-minor (dominant) seventh chords as indicated (root position and all three inversions). Remember that 7 means root position, $^6_5$ means first inversion, $^4_3$ means second inversion, and $^4_2$ means third inversion.

a.

D^4_3 $B\flat^6_5$ C^7 G^4_3 B^4_2 D^7 E^4_2 A^6_5

b.

C^4_2 E^6_5 A^7 D^6_5 B^6_5 F^7 C^4_3 G^4_2

c.

B^7 D^4_2 A^4_3 E^7 G^7 C^6_5 F^4_2 $B\flat^7$

31-6. Use Roman numerals and figured bass numbers to identify these seventh chords in major and minor keys (V^7 and its inversions only). Remember that 7 means root position, $^6_5$ means first inversion, $^4_3$ means second inversion, and $^4_2$ means third inversion. And notice that, in minor keys, scale-degree $\hat{7}$ is raised when forming the dominant seventh chord in all of its positions.

a.

G major: V^6_5 _____   _____   _____

Name: _____

Date: _____

Instructor's Name: _____

b. D minor: ___   ___   ___   ___

c. B♭ major: ___   ___   ___   ___

d. B minor: ___   ___   ___   ___

e. G minor: ___   ___   ___   ___

f. F major: ___   ___   ___   ___

31-7. You are given a major or minor key and a Roman numeral with figured bass numbers. Write the appropriate seventh chord (V^7 and its inversions only). In minor keys, the dominant seventh chord is always made with raised $\hat{7}$ (the leading tone).

a. F: V^6_5 d: V^7 C: V^4_2 e: V^6_5 B♭: V^6_5 G: V^7 a: V^4_3

b. d: V^6_5 E♭: V^6_5 f#: V^6_5 b: V^7 F: V^7 C: V^7 D: V^7

c. D: V^6_5 d: V^4_2 f#: V^7 C: V^4_3 e: V^7 g: V^7 A: V^4_2

d. a: V^7 A: V^7 g: V^4_3 B♭: V^7 b: V^6_5 G: V^4_3 E♭: V^4_2

mysearchlab

31-8. You are given a V⁷ chord (or one of its inversions). Name the tonic note of the key to which it belongs. (The key may be either major or minor.)

mysearchlab

31-9. Use Roman numerals and figured bass numbers to identify triads and seventh chords in these works.

a. Schubert, "Heidenröslein" (this piece begins in one key [G major], moves to another [D major], then returns to where it began. This process is called "modulation." In the second measure, the harmony is an inversion of a seventh chord built on scale-degree 2̂. Each harmony lasts for one full beat and includes both the bass note in the left hand and the chord in the right. To identify the triads and seventh chords, focus on the piano part only, ignoring the notes in parentheses—these serve to decorate or embellish the harmonies. Then, notice the extent to which the melody either reinforces or contradicts the harmony—the contradictory notes, especially if they occur on a beat, have a particular expressive force).

Name: _____

Date: _____

Instructor's Name: _____

war   so   jung   und   mor - gen - schön,   lief   er   schnell   es   nah'___   zu___   sehn,
it was   so   fresh   and   beau - ti - ful   he   ran   quickly   to   gaze___   at___   it,

D major: __IV__   ___   ___ ___ ___

sah's   mit   vie - len   Freu -   den.   Rös - lein,   Rös - lein,   Rös - lein   roth,
gaze   with   great_____   joy._____   Lit - tle   rose,___   little   red   rose,

cresc.   **pp**

___   ___   ___   ___ G major: ___   ___   ___   ___

Rös - lein   auf   der   Hei -   den.
rose___   amid   the   hea - ther.

___   ___   __V__   __I__

b. Rodríguez, "La Cumparsita" (within both tonic and dominant harmonies, the D in the melody is embellished with notes above and below it. Disregard the notes in parentheses).

G minor: ___

c. Lang, Song (one unfamiliar chord—the first inversion of ii7—is identified for you. Ignore the notes in parentheses—they embellish the harmonies you are asked to identify).

Langsam und Ausdrucksvoll (Slowly and expressively)

Ob ich manch-mal dein Ge - den - ke?   wüsst est Du   wie sehr ich's thu!
Do   I some-times think of   you?_____   If on - ly   you knew how much!

E♭ major: ___   ___   ___   ___   ii⁶₅   ___

d. Mendelssohn, Piano Trio (ignore the notes in parentheses—they embellish the harmonies you are asked to identify).

D major: ___   ___   ___   ___   ___   ___

Name: _____

Date: _____

Instructor's Name: _____

e. Chopin, Prelude in A Major (the notes in parentheses embellish
the harmonies. The fact that these embellishing tones occur on the
downbeat gives them particular expressive force).

A major: ___   ___

Chapter 5: Supplementary Lesson

In this lesson you will learn about qualities of seventh chords, natural seventh chords, inversions of seventh chords, and seventh chords in major and minor keys.

The previous lesson focused on the major-minor (dominant) seventh chord. This supplementary lesson gives a full account of seventh chords.

There are five **qualities** of seventh chords in common use (illustrated   Qualities
here with D as their root).

	Full name:	Major-major	Major-minor	Minor-minor	Diminished-minor	Diminished-diminished
	Common name:	Major	Dominant	Minor	Half-diminished	Fully diminished
Five kinds of seventh chords	Chord symbol:	D^{maj7}	D^7	Dm^7	D^{ø7}	D^{o7}
	Triad quality:	M	M	m	d	d
	Seventh quality:	M	m	m	m	d

It is possible to write seven different seventh chords without any accidentals—these are the **natural seventh chords**.

Natural seventh chords

Natural seventh chords

| MM | mm | mm | MM | Mm | mm | dm |

| C^{maj7} | Dm^7 | Em^7 | F^{maj7} | G^7 | Am^7 | B^{ø7} |

All seventh chords involve these seven stacks of letter names: C–E–G–B, D–F–A–C, E–G–B–D, F–A–C–E, G–B–D–F, A–C–E–G, and B–D–F–A. Adding accidentals will change the quality of these natural seventh chords.

The natural seventh chords can also be visualized around a circle of thirds: each natural seventh chord consists of four consecutive notes of the circle.

When talking about seventh chords within a key, Roman numerals with figured bass can be used either instead of or along with the system of alphabetic chord symbols. Just as with triads, the dominant and leading-tone seventh chords in minor are normally made by raising scale-degree $\hat{7}$.

Naming seventh chords in C major

Any seventh chord can appear in inversion as well as root position. The figured bass works as follows: 7 for root position, $\frac{6}{5}$ for first inversion, $\frac{4}{3}$ for second inversion, and $\frac{4}{2}$ for third inversion. Here are the five kinds of seventh chords in all four positions with D as the root.

Figured bass

Chord symbols are also useful for indicating inversion: the actual bass note is shown after a slash.

Chord symbols

All of these seventh chords and all of these inversions are not equally common in musical practice, although it is hard to generalize. For examples of seventh chords of different kinds in music, return to Exercises 27-6d and 28-4a. Both contain seventh chords that you were previously asked to disregard. Try to identify those seventh chords with the appropriate chord symbol.

Chapter 5: Self-Test

1. Identify the quality of these triads (d = diminished, m = minor, M = major).

2. Write the requested triad.

3. You are given a key and a triad or seventh chord. Provide the appropriate Roman numeral and figured bass.

4. You are given a key and a Roman numeral with figured bass. Write the requested triad or seventh chord.

G: V   e:ii°⁶   c: III   g: V   A: IV   E♭: I⁶

d: i⁶   B♭: V⁷   D: V⁶   b: vii°⁶   f: iv⁶   E: V⁶

Chapter 5: Self-Test (answer key)

1. Identify the quality of these triads (d = diminished, m = minor, M = major).

2. Write the requested triad.

3. You are given a key and a triad or seventh chord. Provide the appropriate Roman numeral and figured bass.

4. You are given a key and a Roman numeral with figured bass. Write the requested triad or seventh chord.

G: V   e: ii°⁶   c: III   g: V   A: IV   E♭: I⁶

d: i⁶   B♭: V⁷   D: V⁶   b: vii°⁶   f: iv⁶   E: V⁶

6 *Fundamentals of Harmony*

Lesson 32: Tonic and dominant

In this lesson you will learn about harmonic progression, tonic harmony, dominant and dominant seventh harmonies, and harmonizing a melody.

A **harmonic progression** is a succession of harmonies in which each leads purposefully to the next. Each harmony has its own distinctive character and its own role to play. The **tonic harmony** generally conveys a feeling of stability and repose. Progressions often start on the tonic and very often end on it. Normally, tonal motion is directed toward the tonic as a goal.

Harmonic progression

Tonic harmony

The main function of the **dominant harmony** is to lead to the tonic. Indeed, the most basic harmonic progression involves three chords: I–V–I. It begins on the tonic (in a state of poised repose), moves to the dominant (which has a strong tendency to move to the tonic), and concludes on the tonic (conveying a sense of arrival and completion).

Dominant harmony

I–V–I

C major: I V I   A minor: i V i

The progression I-V-I is often written in this standard, conventional way. Each triad is written in four **voices**: a soprano (the highest-sounding note in each chord, written on the treble staff with an upward stem); an alto and a tenor (the next highest notes, written on the treble staff with a shared downward stem); and a bass (the lowest note, written by itself on the bass staff). Because triads contain three notes but are conventionally written in four voices, one note in each triad is **doubled** (i.e., occurs two times). This arrangement of notes on the great staff—with three voices in the treble clef and one in the bass clef—is often called **keyboard style**, because it is particularly easy to read and play at the keyboard.

Voices

Doubling

Keyboard style

The progression I–V–I can be intensified by adding the interval of a seventh above the root of the dominant triad—that turns the dominant triad into a **dominant seventh chord**. The tendency of the dominant to resolve to the tonic is strengthened by the presence of the dissonant seventh.

Dominant seventh chord

I–V⁷–I

C major: I V⁷ I   A minor: i V⁷ i

The presence of the seventh makes the V⁷ chord dissonant and tense—more eager to resolve to the tonic. The seventh of the V⁷ chord (scale-degree $\hat{4}$) usually resolves down by step to the third of the tonic triad (scale-degree $\hat{3}$). In writing the progression I–V–I in four parts, the root of the chords (scale-degree $\hat{1}$ for I and scale-degree $\hat{5}$ for V) is usually doubled. In writing V⁷, it is sometimes convenient to leave the chord incomplete by omitting the fifth of the chord (scale-degree $\hat{2}$) and doubling the root (scale-degree $\hat{5}$). The general rule of doubling is: never double a tone that has a strong tendency. In V and V⁷, that means never doubling the leading tone (scale-degree $\hat{7}$)—it has a strong tendency to resolve upward to the tonic—and never doubling the chordal seventh (scale-degree $\hat{4}$)—it has a strong tendency to resolve down to the third of the tonic triad.

Harmonization   Many melodies can be **harmonized** using the tonic and dominant harmonies (I and V or V⁷). To harmonize a melody, follow these steps (illustrated with four different melodic fragments in the key of D major).

1. Identify the scale degree of each melody note and figure out if it belongs to the tonic triad (scale-degrees $\hat{1}$–$\hat{3}$–$\hat{5}$), the dominant triad (scale-degrees $\hat{5}$–$\hat{7}$–$\hat{2}$), the dominant seventh chord (scale-degrees $\hat{5}$–$\hat{7}$–$\hat{2}$–$\hat{4}$), or more than one of these. (Notice that scale-degree is the only one shared by tonic and dominant harmonies.)

Identify possible chords

2. Choose a good, strong progression of harmonies and write the bass line. For now, we will define a strong progression of harmonies as one that begins on I and ends either V–I or V⁷–I.

Write the bass line

3. Add inner voices (alto and tenor) to fill out the chords.

Fill in inner voices

Here is a simple way of realizing the progression I–V⁷–I that makes it particularly easy to play at the keyboard.

Keyboard realization

$$I \quad V^7 \quad I$$

These left-hand chords can be used to harmonize melodies that are played by the right hand or sung.

Harmonizing
at the keyboard

When you use this keyboard realization of I–V⁷–I, you may end up creating problems with the relations among the voices (see Chapter 6: Supplementary lesson for details). As a result, your instructor may choose to advise you against it, and to skip the keyboard exercises based on it.

Lesson 32: In-class activities

1. **Singing.** Sing these melodies, using a neutral syllable like "la," solfège syllables, or scale-degree numbers. Think about the harmonies and the harmonic progression that each melody outlines. Transpose to other keys. Melodies e and f below work well as a four-part round.

2. Singing (improvise). Improvise melodies that arpeggiate tonic and dominant, beginning and ending on the tonic. Here are two samples:

3. Singing. Sing these short four-voice chorales. Students should have the opportunity to sing each of the parts.

4. Dictation. The instructor will play a major or minor scale to establish a context, followed by I, V, or V^7. Identify the chord you hear.

5. Dictation. The instructor will play these three-chord progressions in a random order within each group. All of the progressions include only I and V or V^7, all in root position. Identify each progression and the chords it contains.

6. Playing. Play the following progressions. Transpose to other keys.

7. Playing. Harmonize these short melodies by adding three lower voices.

Name: _____

Date: _____

Instructor's Name: _____

LESSON 32: EXERCISES

32-1. Using only I and V or V⁷, harmonize these short melodic fragments (derived from works in the anthology). Supply one chord for each note in the melody, and identify each chord with a Roman numeral (some chords and Roman numerals are provided for you). The melody note you are given should be the highest note in each chord. Try to move the voices as smoothly as possible (avoid large leaps). When you have harmonized a melody, transpose what you have written to a different key, as indicated. Play what you have written at the piano before handing it in—be sure it sounds the way you want it to. After you have finished, compare your work with the actual music from which the melody is adapted.

Remember the three-step procedure for harmonizing a melody:

1. Identify the scale degree of each melody note and figure out if it belongs to the tonic triad (scale-degrees $\hat{1}$–$\hat{3}$–$\hat{5}$), the dominant triad (scale-degrees $\hat{5}$–$\hat{7}$–$\hat{2}$), the dominant seventh chord (scale-degrees $\hat{5}$–$\hat{7}$–$\hat{2}$–$\hat{4}$), or more than one of these.

2. Choose a good, strong progression of harmonies and write the bass line.

3. Add inner voices (alto and tenor) to fill out the chords.

   a. Chopin, Prelude in A Major, mm. 1–8 (every two measures in the music are represented by one measure in this exercise).

A major: V   B♭ major:

   b. Arlen, "Over the Rainbow," mm. 9–11.

E♭ major: I   D major:

c. Ellington, "It Don't Mean a Thing," mm. 26–29.

G minor: V   V₇   E minor:

d. Chopin, Prelude in C minor, m. 1.

C minor: i   V⁷   B minor:

e. Joplin, "The Entertainer," mm. 5–8.

C major: I   F major:

f. Schubert, "Death and the Maiden," mm. 1–4.

D minor: i   E minor:

g. Handy, "St. Louis Blues," mm. 33–40 (despite the key signature, this passage is in G minor).

G minor: i

Name: _____

Date: _____

Instructor's Name: _____

A major:

    h. Mozart, "Dove sono," mm. 1–8.

C major: I   I   I   V^7

B♭ major:

32-2. Using only I and V or V^7, add three upper voices for the following bass lines (derived from works in the anthology). Supply one chord for each bass note and identify each chord with a Roman numeral (some chords and Roman numerals are provided for you). Try to move the voices as smoothly as possible (avoid large leaps). Play what you have written at the piano before handing it in—be sure it sounds the way you want it to. After you have finished, compare your work with the actual music from which the melody is adapted.

    a. Chopin, Prelude in A Major, mm. 1–8 (condensed).

A major: V

b. Arlen, "Over the Rainbow," mm. 9–11.

E♭ major: I

c. Ellington, "It Don't Mean a Thing," mm. 27–30.

G minor: i

d. Chopin, Prelude in C minor, m. 1.

C minor: i

e. Schubert, "Death and the Maiden," mm. 1–4.

D minor: i   i

f. Haydn, String Quartet, mm. 48–56.

C major: I

Name: _____

Date: _____

Instructor's Name: _____

g. Mozart, "Dove sono," mm. 1–8.

C major: I   I   I

32-3. Identify the boxed chords as I, V, or V⁷. All nine passages end with the
same two chords—a dominant followed by a tonic. Think about why
that should be so.

a. Schubert, "Death and the Maiden" (the third and eighth chords are
incomplete, but you should be able to figure them out even with
one note omitted).

D minor: __   __   __   __   __   __   __   __   __

b. Joplin, "The Entertainer."

C major: __   __   __

c. Bach, Chorale (this is the concluding phrase of the chorale).

E♭ major: __   __   __

d. Ellington, "It Don't Mean a Thing."

It   don't mean a   thing,   if it   ain't   got that   swing.____

G minor: __   __   __   __

e. Lang, Song.

Ob   ich manch-mal dein Ge - den   -   ke?   wüsst est Du   wie sehr ich's thu!
*Do   I   some - times think of you?*____   *If   on - ly   you knew how much!*

E♭ major: __   __   __

Name: _____

Date: _____

Instructor's Name: _____

    f. Chopin, Prelude in C minor.

C minor: ___   ___   ___

    g. Chopin, Prelude in A Major (the entire piece, like this passage, consists
       of an alternation of tonic and dominant harmonies).

A major: ___   ___

    ___   ___

h. Handy, "St. Louis Blues" (despite the key signature, this passage is in G minor, and the piece as a whole moves back and forth constantly between G major and G minor).

G minor:

i. Rodríguez, "La Cumparsita" (like many popular dances, this tango consists largely of tonic and dominant harmonies).

G minor:

Name: _____

Date: _____

Instructor's Name: _____

Lesson 33: Expanding I and V

In this lesson you will learn about embellishment and prolongation (nonharmonic tones), passing tones, neighboring tones, passing chords (V_3^4 and vii^{o6}), neighboring chords (V^6, V_5^6, V_2^4, and IV), I^6, and the cadential $^6_4$.

The tonic and dominant harmonies, and any other harmonies, may be **embellished** with foreign notes. These decorative, **embellishing tones** are always just one step away from a note that does belong to a harmony, and they have the effect of **prolonging** or extending a harmony. They often are called **nonharmonic tones**.

There are two main types of embellishing notes: **passing tones** and **neighboring tones**. A passing tone fills in the space between two harmonic tones. It may be ascending or descending, accented or unaccented.

Embellishment

Prolongation
Nonharmonic tones
Passing tones
Neighboring tones

Passing tones

Unlike a passing tone, which connects two different tones, a neighboring tone moves away from and back to a single, stationary tone. A neighbor may occur above (upper neighbor) or below (lower neighbor) and it may be accented or unaccented.

Neighboring tones

Incomplete neighboring tones

These neighboring tones are **complete**: they depart from and return to a harmonic tone. Neighboring tones also can be **incomplete**, attached to a harmonic tone before or after, but not both.

Just as individual tones may have a passing or neighboring function with respect to other tones, entire harmonies may have a passing or neighboring function with respect to other harmonies. The second inversion of the V^7 chord (V_3^4), for example, is often used as a passing chord to connect I with I^6. Its bass note, scale-degree $\hat{2}$ acts as a passing tone: it comes by step from I and continues by step to I^6. In addition, vii^{o6} has the same bass note and often has the same passing function.

Passing chords
(V_3^4 and vii^{o6})

The first inversion of the dominant or dominant seventh chords (V^6 and V^6_5) is often used as a **neighboring chord** to connect two statements of I. The leading tone in the bass acts as a **neighboring tone**: the bass of the I chord moves down a step to the bass of V^6 or V^6_5 then right back to its starting point.

Neighboring chords
(V^6 and V^6_5)

I V^6 I   I V^6_5 I

In a somewhat different sense, the subdominant triad (IV) can also function as a neighboring chord to I. The common progression I–IV–I prolongs the tonic harmony and the IV chord frequently supports a melodic neighboring tone, either $\hat{3}$–$\hat{4}$–$\hat{3}$ or $\hat{5}$–$\hat{6}$–$\hat{5}$.

Neighboring chords (IV)

I   IV   I   I   IV   I

So far all of the passing and neighboring chords we have discussed are used to embellish or prolong tonic harmony. But the dominant can also be embellished. One particularly common kind of embellishment involves preceding the third and fifth of the dominant triad with their upper neighbors. This produces a chord that looks like the second inversion of a tonic triad (I^6_4) but functions as an embellishment of the dominant. This is called the **cadential** $^6_4$ because it frequently occurs at cadences.

cadential

Cadential $^6_4$

I   V   I

Lesson 33: In-class activities

1. Singing. Sing these melodies, which elaborate a tonic triad with passing and neighboring tones. Identify all nonharmonic tones as either passing or neighboring. Transpose to other keys.

a.

b.

c.

d.

2. **Singing.** Sing these melodies, which elaborate tonic and dominant harmonies. Identify all nonharmonic tones (circled on the music) as passing or neighboring.

a. Joplin, "The Entertainer" (some of the embellishing tones are *diatonic*—they use notes within the scale—and some are *chromatic*—they use notes with sharps or flats that lie outside the scale).

b. Mozart, "Dove sono" (the first, second, and fourth dominant chords are embellished with an accented passing tone. The third dominant chord includes a seventh [F]).

c. Rodríguez, "La Cumparsita" (a melodic figure that contains both upper and lower neighbors is called a **double neighbor**).

d. Haydn, String Quartet (here is another double neighbor, but the second one is incomplete).

e. Schubert, "Death and the Maiden" (the first two measures span the interval of a third, D–F, within the tonic harmony. The third measure also spans a third, but within the dominant harmony, E–C♯).

f. Chopin, Prelude in A Major (the D in parentheses in the first measure is a neighbor to C♯, which is itself a neighbor to B).

3. Singing. Sing these melodies, which arpeggiate progressions that contain passing or neighboring chords.

4. **Singing.** Sing these duets with one student or group of students on a part; then switch parts. Identify the circled notes as passing or neighboring. Notice that dissonant intervals occur only on the second beat of the measure and only as passing or neighboring tones; the note on the first beat is always consonant.

5. **Singing.** Sing these duets. They involve neighboring and passing harmonies—try to identify them. After you have sung them, compare the duets to the music from which they are adapted.

a. Lang, Song, mm. 1–4 (adapted)

b. Mendelssohn, Piano Trio, mm. 1–3 (adapted)

6. **Singing.** Sing these two passages as a vocal quartet. Only tonic and dominant harmonies are used; identify all nonharmonic tones as either passing or neighboring.

a. Schubert, "Death and the Maiden," mm. 1–8 (this passage is the piano introduction to the song. It sounds like a dirge in D minor and it represents the character of Death).

b. Schubert, "Death and the Maiden," mm. 37–43 (this passage is the piano postlude to the song. It takes the music from the beginning and shifts it from D minor to D major. Death has triumphed).

7. Dictation. The instructor will play these short progressions in a random order within each group. Identify the progression. The progressions in Group 1 involve passing and neighboring tones; the progressions in Group 2 involve passing and neighboring harmonies.

8. Playing. Play these progressions that elaborate tonic and dominant harmonies with passing or neighboring notes. Transpose to other keys.

9. Playing. Play these progressions, which involve passing or neighboring harmonies. Transpose them to other keys.

10. Playing. Improvise short melodies with your right hand while playing these chords with your left. Try to play steadily with a definite rhythm. The melodies you play will use the tones of the chords, and embellish those tones with passing and neighboring tones. If you wish, you may sing rather than play your melody.

Example: (three melodies for chord progression a.)

Name: _____

Date: _____

Instructor's Name: _____

LESSON 33: EXERCISES

33-1. Compose duets by completing a melody above the given melody. On the second half of each measure, add a half note that is a passing tone or a neighboring tone. Play each duet at the piano before handing it in—be sure it sounds the way you want it to. Be prepared to sing both the melody you are given and the melody you have written in class.

33-2. Identify the circled notes as passing or neighboring by writing P or N directly above each note (some are done for you). Remember that a passing tone connects two harmonic tones that lie a third apart (it involves two steps in the same direction) while a neighbor tone departs from and/or returns to a single note.

a. Mozart, Sonata (for most of the passage, the bass and soprano move together in parallel motion).

b. Haydn, String Quartet (accented, incomplete lower neighbor tones are featured first as part of the descending line in the highest voice and then in the ascending line in the lowest voice).

c. Arlen, "Over the Rainbow" (the prevailing harmony is E♭ major—only one note does not belong).

Where troubles melt like lemon drops, a -

d. Schubert, "Death and the Maiden" (there is only one harmony in each measure—the notes that don't belong to the harmony are neighboring or passing tones. The double-neighbor figure—a four-note figure that starts on the main note, continues with its upper and lower neighbors, then returns to the main note—is used in measures 1 and 5).

Name: _____

Date: _____

Instructor's Name: _____

e. Mozart, Sonata (the bass line arpeggiates the harmony—either tonic or dominant. The melody embellishes those harmonies with passing and neighboring tones, including the double-neighbor figure).

f. Handy, "St. Louis Blues" (in measure 2, the passing tone C♯ connects the harmony tone C with its upper neighbor D. The key signature tells us this piece as a whole is in G major, but this passage is in G minor).

man roun'_____   by her a-pron   strings_____

33-3. Compose a melody for each of these chord progressions (involving tonic and dominant only). The melodies you write will use the tones of the chords, and embellish those tones with passing and neighboring tones. See In-class activity 33-10 for some examples. Play your compositions on the piano before handing them in—be sure they sound the way you want them to. When you use the arrangement of harmonies in Exercises 33-3 and 33-4, with three voices close together in the bass clef, you may end up creating problems with the relations among the voices (see Chapter 6: Supplementary lesson for details). As a result, your instructor may choose to skip these exercises.

a.

b.

c.

d.

Name: _____

Date: _____

Instructor's Name: _____

33-4. Harmonize these melodies by adding three-note chords in the bass **mysearchlab** clef (tonic and dominant only). Some chords are provided for you. Begin by singing the melody several times to become familiar with it. Try to figure out what harmonies it suggests and which of its notes are nonharmonic tones.

a. Arlen, "Over the Rainbow."

b. Chopin, Prelude in A Major.

c. Haydn, String Quartet (adapted).

d. Joplin, "The Entertainer."

e. Mendelssohn, Piano Trio.

f. Rodríguez, "La Cumparsita."

g. Schubert, "Death and the Maiden."

mysearchlab   33-5. Use Roman numerals and figured-bass numbers to identify harmonies. They are either passing harmonies (like V_3^4 and $vii°^6$) or neighboring harmonies (like V^6, V_5^6 or IV).

a. Handy, "St. Louis Blues" (both the tonic harmony and the neighboring harmony that prolongs it are heavily embellished with passing and neighboring notes. The tonic harmony in measure 1 has a seventh [F] added to it).

b. Haydn, String Quartet (the tonic is elaborated by a neighboring harmony. Despite the key signature, this passage is in A major).

A: I   I ii^6 V

c. Mendelssohn, Piano Trio (the tonic harmony at the beginning and end of the passage is prolonged by neighboring harmonies that involve both an upper neighbor [E] and a lower neighbor [C♯] in the bass).

Name: _____

Date: _____

Instructor's Name: _____

D: I   I

d. Lang, Song (a passing chord connects I with I⁶).

Ob   ich manch - mal   dein   Ge - den - ke?
Do   I   some - times   think   of   you? _____

E♭:   I   I⁶

e. Schubert, "Death and the Maiden" (the passing chord that connects
  I with I⁶ is actually a seventh chord, not a triad. Its root is C#—ignore
  the seventh [B♭] in labeling it).

  Das Mädchan (The Maiden)

Vor - ü - ber,   ach, vor - ü - ber!   geh,   wil - der Kno - chen - mann!
Pass   by,_____   ah,   pass   by!_____   Go,   harsh,_____ bo - ny Death!

d: i   i⁶

mysearchlab 33-6. Harmonize these melodies by adding three lower voices. The notes of the melody you are given should be the highest in each chord. Roman numerals and some bass notes are provided. Play your compositions before handing them in—be sure they sound the way you want them to. When you have finished, compare your work to the passages from which these melodies are adapted.

a. Schubert, "Death and the Maiden," mm. 18–19.

b. Mozart, Sonata, mm. 1–4.

c. Lang, Song, mm. 1–3.

d. Handy, "St. Louis Blues," mm. 9–11.

e. Mendelssohn, Piano Trio, mm. 1–5.

Lesson 34: Approaching V

In this lesson you will learn about dominant preparation chords (ii and IV).

Just as the dominant leads to the tonic, there are harmonies that lead to the dominant. Chords like these are called **dominant preparation** or **predominant** chords, and the most important are ii and IV.

Dominant preparation
Predominant

In the progression from ii to V, the bass moves up by a fourth or down by a fifth. That is a very strong kind of harmonic motion, imitating the motion from V to I. (Note that ii in root position rarely occurs in minor keys because composers generally avoid writing diminished triads in root position.)

ii–V

descending 5th

I   ii   V   I

In first inversion, ii⁶ works well in major and minor. Its bass note is scale-degree $\hat{4}$ which moves smoothly by step as ii⁶ progresses to V.

ii⁶–V

ascending step   ascending step

I   ii⁶   V   I   i   ii°⁶   V   i

IV has the same bass note as ii⁶, and when it moves to V, its bass also moves smoothly by step. Like ii⁶, IV acts as a neighboring chord to V, approaching it from a step below.

IV–V

ascending step   ascending step

I   IV   V   I   i   iv   V   i

IV thus has two different roles: sometimes it leads to I (discussed in Lesson 33) and sometimes it leads to V (as a dominant preparation chord). Dominant preparation chords (ii, ii⁶, and IV) can also lead to V⁶ or to the dominant seventh chord in any of its positions.

Here is a simple way of realizing the progression I–IV–V⁷–I that makes it particularly easy to play at the keyboard.

Keyboard
realization

I   IV   V⁷   I   i   iv   V⁷   i

In this arrangement, the progression can be played with the left hand alone, and used to harmonize melodies that are either played by the right hand or sung. When you use this keyboard realization, you may end up creating problems with the relations among the voices (see Chapter 6: Supplementary lesson for details). As a result, your instructor may choose to advise you against it, and to skip the keyboard exercises based on it.

Lesson 34: In-class activities

1. **Singing.** Sing these melodies, which arpeggiate progressions involving dominant preparation chords. Identify the harmonies. Transpose to other keys.

2. **Singing.** Sing these four-part chorales, with one student or group of students to a part. Identify the harmonies.

   a. Bach, Chorale (here are two different harmonizations of the same melody—it is the last phrase of the chorale).

b. Mozart, "Dove sono," mm. 1–8 (after you have sung this vocal quartet, compare it to the passage from which it is adapted).

c. Haydn, String Quartet, mm. 77–92 (after you have sung this vocal quartet, compare it to the passage from which it is adapted).

3. Dictation. The instructor will play four-chord progressions in a random order within each group. Some involve dominant preparation chords and some do not. Identify the progression.

4. Playing. Play these progressions. Transpose to other keys.

C: I   ii⁶   V⁷   I   a: i   ii°⁶   V⁷   i

C: I   IV   V⁷   I   a: i   iv   V⁷   i

5. Playing. Harmonize these short melodies by adding three lower voices.

Example:

(D major)

or

a.

(G minor)

b.

(A major)

c.

(F major)

d.

(E minor)

e.

(E♭ major)

6. Playing. Improvise melodies with your right hand while playing these chords with your left. Try to play steadily with a definite rhythm. The melodies you play will use the tones of the chords, and embellish those tones with passing and neighboring notes. See In-class activity 33-10 for examples. You may wish to sing rather than play your melody.

a.

b.

c.

Name: _____

Date: _____

Instructor's Name: _____

LESSON 34: EXERCISES

34-1. Harmonize these melodies by adding three lower voices. The notes of the melody you are given should be the highest in each chord. Roman numerals and some bass notes are provided. Play your compositions before handing them in—be sure they sound the way you want them to. When you have finished, compare your work to the passages from which these melodies are adapted.

   a. Handy, "St. Louis Blues," mm. 1–7 (many other passages use a similar melodic and harmonic framework).

   b. Mozart, Sonata, mm. 17–18.

   c. Chopin, Prelude in A Major (adapted).

d. Chopin, Prelude in C minor, m. 1 (the F after the third beat is a passing tone).

c: i   iv   V   i

e. Haydn, String Quartet, mm. 2–5 (adapted. The F in measure 3 is a passing tone).

C: I   ii ⁶   V   I

mysearchlab 34-2. Use Roman numerals to identify the harmonies in these works.

a. Schumann, Song (this phrase moves from an initial tonic to a concluding dominant, which is preceded by a dominant preparation chord).

Wenn ich in dei - ne   Au - ge seh',   so   then   scwhindet all' mein Leid und   Weh;
When I in - to your   *eyes__ look,*   *so*   *then* *fades__ all my pain and*   *sorrow;*

G: __   __   __   __   __

b. Bach, Chorale (in the sixth and seventh chords, the alto voice has an accented dissonance—ignore those notes in your identification of the chords).

D: __   __   __   __   __

Name: _____

Date: _____

Instructor's Name: _____

c. Haydn, **String Quartet** (the fourth chord represents an arrival on the tonic, but it is embellished by accented neighbor notes in both soprano [first violin] and tenor [viola]).

C: ⎯   ⎯   ⎯   ⎯

d. Schubert, "Heidenröslein" (on the first beat of the fourth and sixth measures, the dominant is embellished by the cadential $^6_4$).

G: ⎯   ⎯   ⎯   ⎯   ⎯   ⎯   ⎯   ⎯   ⎯

e. Mozart, "Dove sono" (this passage has a noble simplicity—it uses the simplest harmonies and only the seven notes of the C major scale).

C: ⎯   ⎯   ⎯   ⎯   ⎯   ⎯

f. Mendelssohn, Piano Trio (the last four measures of the piece are all tonic—but the tonic is extensively embellished with neighbor and passing tones, and with one neighboring chord).

Name: _____

Date: _____

Instructor's Name: _____

g. Handy, "St. Louis Blues" (in this piece, the subdominant is often used as a neighboring chord to prolong the tonic, but in the second measure of this passage, it is a dominant preparation chord).

h. Mozart, "Dove sono" (V usually resolves to I, but in this passage it is often diverted to vi instead as a way of building tension and anticipation for the final blazing tonic arrival).

Name: _____

Date: _____

Instructor's Name: _____

i. Joplin, "The Entertainer" (there are only three harmonies in this passage, with the second acting as a neighbor to the third).

C: __   __   __

34-3. Compose a melody for each of these chord progressions (involving I, IV, and V⁷ only). The melodies you write will use the tones of the chords, and embellish those tones with passing and neighboring tones. Play your compositions on the piano before handing them in—be sure they sound the way you want them to. See In-class activity 33-10 for examples.

a.

b.

c.

Lesson 35: Phrase and cadence

In this lesson you will learn about phrase, authentic cadence, half cadence, period (antecedent and consequent), and plagal cadence.

A **phrase** in music is like a sentence in language: a self-contained utterance with a beginning, middle, and end. Phrases in music are groups of measures, often groups of two, four, or eight measures. Like sentences, musical phrases end with a form of punctuation—in language the punctuation is a period; in music it is called a **cadence**.

Phrase

Cadence

There are two principal types of cadences: authentic cadences and half cadences. An **authentic cadence** involves a progression from dominant to tonic (V–I), providing a strong sense of arrival on the tonic at the end of a phrase. The V–I progression can occur anywhere in a phrase; only when it occurs at the end of a phrase is it called an authentic cadence. Musical phrases vary considerably in length and content, but a particularly common arrangement is a four-measure phrase that begins on the tonic and ends with an authentic cadence.

Authentic cadence

Four-measure phrase
with authentic cadence

Here are five different realizations of that prototype:

a. Joplin, "The Entertainer."

b. Lang, Song.

Ob ich manch-mal dein Ge - den - ke? ... wüsst est Du wie sehr ich's thu!
Do I some - times think of you? _____ ... *If on - ly you knew how much!*

c. Ellington, "It Don't Mean a Thing."

d. Haydn, String Quartet.

e. Chopin, Prelude in C minor.

Half cadence

The second principal type of cadence is the **half cadence**, which involves an arrival on the dominant (V). Because the dominant has a more tense, unresolved quality than the tonic, a half cadence does not sound like a definitive ending, more like a temporary pause in the musical flow (more like a comma or even a question mark than a period). A common arrangement is a four-measure phrase that begins on the tonic and ends on the dominant.

Four-measure phrase with half cadence

Here are three realizations of that prototype.

a. Schumann, Song.

b. Mozart, Sonata.

c. Ellington, "It Don't Mean a Thing."

Longer phrases are created by combining shorter ones. An eight-measure phrase, for example, might result from a combination of two four-measure phrases, and might combine with another eight-measure phrase to create a sixteen-measure phrase—these larger combinations are called **periods**. A particularly common arrangement involves one phrase that ends with a half cadence followed by another that ends on the tonic. When these two balanced phrases begin in the same way, the first is called an **antecedent** and the second is called a **consequent**, while their combination is called a **parallel period**. Here are two parallel periods:

Period

Antecedent
Consequent
Parallel period

a. Mozart, Sonata.

b. Haydn, String Quartet.

Plagal cadence   There is one additional type of cadence that occurs from time to time, although not nearly as often as the authentic and half cadences. The **plagal cadence** involves a progression from subdominant to tonic (IV–I). The subdominant has none of the strong pull toward the tonic that the dominant has. As a result, the plagal cadence is weaker than the authentic cadence and, in fact, usually occurs after an authentic cadence as a kind of extra confirmation. Here is one example:

Schumann, Song

Lesson 35: In-class activities

1. **Singing.** Sing the following melodies and identify the type of cadence, marked with an arrow (authentic or half). Authentic cadences usually end with scale-degree $\hat{1}$ in the melody, or occasionally with scale-degree $\hat{3}$ (over the tonic harmony). Half cadences usually have scale-degree $\hat{2}$ in the melody, or occasionally scale-degree $\hat{5}$ or $\hat{7}$ (over the dominant harmony).

a. Arlen, "Over the Rainbow."

b. Ellington, "It Don't Mean a Thing."

There's some-thing else that makes the   tune   com - plete.

c. Ellington, "It Don't Mean a Thing."

It   don't mean a   thing, if   it   ain't   got that   swing. _

d. Haydn, String Quartet (this is a parallel period).

e. Haydn, String Quartet.

f. Joplin, "The Entertainer."

g. Mozart, Sonata (this is a parallel period).

h. Mozart, "Dove sono" (this is a parallel period, with the second phrase stretched out to ten measures compared to the eight measures of the first phrase).

i. Schubert, "Death and the Maiden."

2. Dictation. The instructor will play four-chord progressions in a random order within each group. Identify the progression you hear and describe the type of cadence with which it ends (authentic, half, or plagal).

Group 1

Group 2

3. Playing. Improvise melodies with your right hand while playing these chords with your left. Try to play steadily with a definite rhythm. The melodies you play will use the tones of the chords, and embellish those tones with passing and neighboring notes. See In-class activity 33-10 for examples. You may wish to sing rather than play your melody.

a. Four-measure phrase ending with an authentic cadence.

b. Four-measure phrase ending with a half cadence.

c. Parallel period (your melody for measures 1–2 should be the same as for measures 5–6).

Name: _____

Date: _____

Instructor's Name: _____

LESSON 35: EXERCISES

35-1. In the following passages, cadences are marked with an arrow. Identify them as authentic or half cadences.

a. Arlen, "Over the Rainbow."

b. Handy, "St. Louis Blues."

c. Mozart, Sonata (the piece is divided into four-measure phrases, each punctuated with a cadence, and with two extra measures added at the end).

d. Rodríguez, "La Cumparsita."

Name: _____

Date: _____

Instructor's Name: _____

e. Joplin, "The Entertainer."

f. Schubert, "Death and the Maiden."
Etwas geschwinder (Somewhat faster)
Das Mädchen (The Maiden)

an,   und   rüh - re mich nicht   an.
me,   and   do   not touch____   me.

35-2. Compose a melody for each of these chord progressions (involving authentic and half cadences). The melodies you write will use the tones of the chords in the left hand, and embellish those tones with passing and neighboring tones. Play your compositions on the piano before handing them in—be sure they sound the way you want them to. See In-class activity 33-10 for examples.

a. Four-measure phrase ending with an authentic cadence.

b. Four-measure phrase ending with a half cadence.

c. Parallel period (your melody for measures 1–2 should be the same as for measures 5–6).

Chapter 6: Supplementary Lesson

In this lesson, you will learn about doubling, voice leading, smoothness, tendency tones, resolution of the seventh, parallel fifths, and octaves.

Triads have only three different notes, but composers often write chords that have four or more notes. As a result, one or more notes of the triad must be **doubled** (i.e., played more than once in the chord). Any note may be doubled **with one important** exception: Tones that have a strong **tendency to resolve in** a particular way (**tendency tones**) are not doubled. The **leading tone**, which occurs as the third of the dominant chord, is such a tendency tone and should not be doubled.

Doubling

Bass doubled
(good)

Leading tone
doubled
(problematic)

The notes of a chord are sometimes called voices: the highest note is the soprano, the second highest is the alto, the third highest is the tenor, and the lowest is the bass. The movement of the voices from chord to chord is called **voice leading**. The bass voice often leaps, but the voice leading for the upper three voices is generally **smooth**, with each voice moving by small intervals (usually unisons, seconds, or thirds) to the nearest available position in the next chord.

Voice leading

Smooth voice
leading (good)

Unsmooth
voice leading

Parallel octaves

Parallel fifths

If two voices are an octave apart in one chord, they should not be an octave apart in the next chord. That is called **parallel octaves**, because the two voices are moving in **parallel motion** (in the same direction by the same interval). **Parallel fifths** are similarly avoided. This preference for avoiding parallel perfect consonances is deeply characteristic of classical music, but much less so of popular styles.

Parallel fifths
and octaves
(avoided
by classical
composers)

There are two important conventions governing the treatment of the seventh in seventh chords such as V^7. First, the seventh is a dissonance and thus has a strong tendency to resolve to a consonance. Normally, dissonances resolve downward by step. In this case, the seventh of the V^7 chord is scale-degree $\hat{4}$ —when the V^7 chord moves to I, scale-degree $\hat{4}$ moves down to scale-degree $\hat{3}$ within the tonic chord.

Resolving
the seventh
(down by step)

Second, because the seventh has such a strong tendency to resolve, it should not be doubled. In this way, it is just like another tendency tone, the leading-tone.

Anthology

"Over the Rainbow"

Harold Arlen (lyrics by E. Y. Harburg)

Harold Arlen (1905–86) was one of a generation of composers (including Jerome Kern, Irving Berlin, Richard Rodgers, and Cole Porter) responsible for a "Golden Age" in American popular song during the second quarter of the twentieth century. He wrote songs for Broadway musicals and Hollywood films, and many have become standards. "Over the Rainbow" was written for the film *The Wizard of Oz*. In it, the character Dorothy (played by Judy Garland in the film) sings of her longing to escape drought-parched Kansas during the Great Depression to a land where "dreams really do come true." The music is performed in many different ways, but it is presented here as Arlen wrote it, for voice and piano with chord symbols. Because of an improvisatory tradition in jazz and popular music performance, the recorded performance on the CD that accompanies this book may not correspond in all respects to the music printed here.

Over the Rainbow

Music by
Harold Arlen

Lyrics by
E. Y. Harburg

(continued)

(continued)

hap-py lit - tle blue-birds fly be - yond the rain-bow, why oh why can't   I?

Two Fugues from *The Well-Tempered Clavier,* Volume 1 (No. 15 in G Major and No. 16 in G minor)

Johann Sebastian Bach

J. S. Bach (1685–1750) is a dominant figure in the history of Western classical music. He wrote hundreds of works for voices and instruments in countless combinations. His *Well-Tempered Clavier,* Volume 1, was written in 1722 and consists of twenty-four Preludes and Fugues in all the major and minor keys (Volume 2, written later, follows the same plan). It was written for the harpsi-chord, but sounds good on any keyboard instrument. The Fugue in G Major is written for three voices—that is, three distinct musical lines—while the Fugue in G minor is written for four voices.

Fugue No. 15 in G Major

Johann Sebastian Bach

(continued)

Fugue No. 16 in G minor

Johann Sebastian Bach

(continued)

Two Chorales from the *St. Matthew Passion*

Johann Sebastian Bach

Amid the dramatic action of Bach's *St. Matthew Passion* (completed in 1729), the chorus pauses from time to time to sing contemplative chorales—these are hymns for four voices: soprano, alto, tenor, and bass. Five chorales in the *St. Matthew Passion* use a melody composed many years earlier by a composer named Hans Leo Hassler. Each of Bach's harmonizations of this melody is different in interesting ways. Two of the chorales are given here, each in two formats. Version A presents the chorale much as it appears in Bach's original score, with each vocal part on a separate staff. Instruments accompany each part. Beneath the score, there is a figured bass—this is the bass line of the chorale with numbered instructions to a keyboard player for producing appropriate chords. Version B gives the chorale in a compact format with soprano and alto sharing the treble clef and tenor and bass sharing the bass clef and with an English translation suitable for singing.

Chorale No. 1 from the *St. Matthew Passion*

Johann Sebastian Bach

(continued)

blas - sen im letz-ten To - des - stoß, als - denn will ich dich fas - sen in mei - nen Arm und Schoß.

blas - sen im letz-ten To - des - stoß, als - denn will ich dich fas - sen in mei-nen Arm und Schoß.

blas - sen im letz-ten To - des - stoß, als - denn will ich dich fas - sen in mei - nen Arm und Schoß.

blas - sen im letz-ten To - des - stoß, als - denn will ich dich fas - sen in mei - nen Arm und Schoß.

B)

Be - side Thee, Lord, I've tak - en My place for - bid me not! If pain's last pale-ness
Hence will I ne'er be shak - en Though Thou to death be brought.

hold Thee, In ag-o - ny op - pressed, Then, then will I en - fold Thee With - in this arm and breast.

Chorale No. 2 from the *St. Matthew Passion*

Johann Sebastian Bach

(continued)

B)

Com-mit thy ways, O   pil - grim   On   time's dark, storm-y   seas,   Who   mea-sures out their
To Him who or - ders   all   things Through sweet e - ter - ni - ties,

cours - es To clouds, winds, waves be - low; He too will find a   path - way Where-in thy feet may go.

Two Preludes from Opus 28 (No. 7 in A Major and No. 20 in C minor)

Frederic Chopin

Frederic Chopin (1810–49) wrote extensively for the piano. His Preludes (completed in 1839) are a set of twenty-four short piano pieces, one in each of the twelve major and twelve minor keys. In its systematic exploration of all the keys, it recalls *The Well-Tempered Clavier* of J. S. Bach. The composer and pianist Franz Liszt commented on these Preludes: "They are compositions of an order entirely apart: they are not merely, as the title would indicate, introductions to other pieces. Rather, they are themselves poetry. Everything in them seems fresh, elastic, created at the impulse of the moment, abounding with that freedom of expression which is characteristic of works of genius." Each of the Preludes has a distinctive character. The Prelude in A Major sounds like a gentle waltz, while the Prelude in C minor sounds like a funeral march.

Prelude No. 7 in A Major

Frederic Chopin

Prelude No. 20 in C minor

Frederic Chopin

"It Don't Mean a Thing" (If It Ain't Got That Swing)

Edward Kennedy ("Duke") Ellington (lyrics by Irving Mills)

Duke Ellington (1899–1974) is perhaps the most important composer in jazz history. He wrote roughly two thousand works, including hundreds of short instrumental pieces and popular songs. "It Don't Mean a Thing" dates from 1932, toward the beginning of Ellington's most fertile creative period. It was written for and first performed and recorded by Ellington's own big band. This is the original sheet music for voice and piano (with chord symbols). Because of an improvisatory tradition in jazz and popular music performance, the recorded performance on the CD that accompanies this book may not correspond in all respects to the music printed here.

It Don't Mean a Thing (If It Ain't Got That Swing)

Music by
Edward Kennedy ("Duke") Ellington

Lyrics by
Irving Mills

(continued)

(continued)

"St. Louis Blues"

William Christopher (W. C.) Handy

W. C. Handy (1873–1958) is sometimes called the "Father of the Blues." He played a major role in the early popularization and wide dissemination of the blues throughout America and abroad. His early involvement with African-American folk music, especially the newly emerging blues in the Mississippi Delta and Memphis, strongly shaped his own later career as a composer, arranger, and performer. He wrote the "St. Louis Blues," probably his best-known piece, in 1914. Because of an improvisatory tradition in jazz and popular music performance, the recorded performance on the CD that accompanies this book may not correspond in all respects to the music printed here.

St. Louis Blues

William Christopher (W. C.) Handy

(continued)

(continued)

String Quartet, Op. 76, No. 3, third movement (Minuet)

Joseph Haydn

Franz Joseph Haydn (1732–1809) was an amazingly prolific and influential composer, a mentor of Mozart, and a teacher of Beethoven. He is known as the "Father of the String Quartet" because he was the first to write a large number of works for a small ensemble of two violins, viola, and cello. His Opus 76 is a set of six quartets, and the third movement of the third quartet is a Minuet (a stately dance in $\frac{3}{4}$ time). In the published score, each instrument has its own staff (with the viola playing in alto clef), but it is presented here in an arrangement on a single great staff: the violins share the top line and the viola and cello share the bottom.

String Quartet, Opus 76, No. 3, third movement (Minuet)

Franz Joseph Haydn

(continued)

"The Entertainer"

Scott Joplin

Scott Joplin (1867 or 1868–1917) is the preeminent composer of piano ragtime. Joplin tried to effect a fusion of popular ragtime with classical harmony and form. The result was what he called "classic rags." He wrote "The Entertainer" in 1902.

The Entertainer

By Scott Joplin

(continued)

(continued)

"Ob ich manchmal dein Gedenke" (Do I Sometimes Think of You)

Josephine Lang (text by Christian Reinhold Koestlin)

Josephine Lang (1815–80) was an important composer of German art songs (*Lieder*). Felix Mendelssohn praised her "divine genius" and commented: "She has the gift of composing songs and singing them as I have never heard before; it is the most complete musical joy I have ever experienced." She wrote about 150 songs, mostly during the 1830s and 1840s. The song included here was written in 1841 and its poetic text is an ecstatic outpouring of romantic love.

Ob ich manchmal dein Gedenke (Do I Sometimes Think of You)

Music by
Josephine Lang

Text by
Christian Reinhold Koestlin

(continued)

ist____ mein sein!

Ob ich manchmal dein Gedenke?
wüsst est Du wie sehr ich's thu!
Dir auch noch die Schatten lenken träumender
Gedanken zu.
Tag und Nacht, und all Stunden,
O, dies Alles sagt es nicht
    Du seit dem wir uns gefunden
bist's allein was aus mir spricht
    Alles Andre seh ich schwanken um
mich her wie Traum und Schein!
Dein gedenken ist mein Leben!
Dich zu lieben ist mein sein!

Do I sometimes think of you?
If only you knew how much!
Directed to you are the shadows of dreaming thoughts.

Day and night, and at all hours,
oh, I can't express it.
You, since we found each other
    are the only one of whom I speak
All else I see swaying around
    me like dream and illusion!
To think of you is my life!
To love you is my existence!

Fanny Mendelssohn

Fanny Mendelssohn (1805–47) wrote a large body of works, mostly songs and short piano pieces, but including cantatas and orchestral works. Many remain unpublished even today, but the increasing availability of her music has begun to suggest its quality and range. Her Trio for Piano, Violin, and Cello, written in 1846, is one of her finest works.

Lied (Song)

Fanny Mendelssohn

(continued)

(continued)

Piano Sonata in A Major, K. 331, first movement (Theme and Variations 1, 3, and 6)

Wolfgang Amadeus Mozart

Wolfgang Amadeus Mozart (1756–91) managed in his extremely short life to write an astonishing number of masterpieces of every kind, including symphonies, operas, concertos, string quartets, and sonatas. The Piano Sonata in A Major, the eleventh of eighteen piano sonatas, dates from 1778. Its first movement is a theme with six variations, three of which are included here.

Piano Sonata in A Major, K. 331, first movement
(Theme and Variations 1, 3, and 6)

(continued)

VAR. VI

Allegro

(continued)

"Dove sono" (I Remember) from *The Marriage of Figaro*

Wolfgang Amadeus Mozart (libretto by Lorenzo da Ponte)

Mozart's opera *The Marriage of Figaro* was first performed in 1786. Classical opera consists of arias (songs for a solo voice) and ensembles (vocal duets, trios, quartets, etc.) connected by a kind of singing speech called recitative. In the aria reprinted here, the Countess first sings regretfully of her husband's loss of affection for her, then hopefully that she might regain his "faithless heart." The music is presented in *piano-vocal score*, with the orchestral parts arranged for piano.

"Dove sono" (I Remember) from *The Marriage of Figaro*

Wolfgang Amadeus Mozart

15 gner, _ di quel lab - bro men - zo - gner.
    go, _ all were bro - ken _ long a - go.

20 Per-chè mai, _ se in pian - tie in pe - ne per me
    Oh, then why, _ if __ I __ was __ fa - ted From that

24 tut - to si can - giò, per me tut - to si can - giò, la me-
    height of joy to fall, from that height of joy to fall, Must I

fp

28 mo - ria di quel be - ne del mio sen _ non tra - pas - sò, __
    still _ those hap - py _ mo - ments in my hour _ of _ pain re - call? __

(continued)

la __ me - mo - ria di quel ben   non __ tra - pas - sò.
those __ hap-py   mo - ments in my   hour   of __ pain __ re - call.

Do -   ve   so - no   i   bei   mo - men __ ti   di   dol -
I   re - mem - ber days long   de - part - ed,   Days   when

cez - za   e   di __ pia - cer; __   Do -   ve an - da - ro   i
love __   no   end __ could __ know; __   I   re - mem - ber fond

giu - ra - mèn - ti   di   quel __ lab - bro __ men - zo - gner! __
vows   and   fer - vent   All   were __ bro - ken __ long a -   go. __

(continued)

(continued)

gra - to   cor.
heart   re - gain.

"La Cumparsita" (The Little Carnival Parade)

Matos Rodríguez

The tango has its roots in the poor slum areas of nineteenth-century Buenos Aires in Argentina and has since become the most popular Argentine dance of the twentieth century. Matos Rodríguez (1897–1948) wrote "La Cumparsita" (The Little Carnival Parade) in 1916 as a marching song for the Federation of Students in Uruguay, of which he was a member. The song was later arranged as a tango by the composer and bandleader Roberto Firpo, and is probably the most famous tango ever written. It has since been rearranged countless times, but is provided here in the form in which it was first published, for piano and violin. Because of an improvisatory tradition in jazz and popular music performance, the recorded performance on the CD that accompanies this book may not correspond in all respects to the music printed here.

La Cumparsita (The Little Carnival Parade)

Matos Rodríguez

(continued)

Two Songs: "Der Tod und das Mädchen" (Death and the Maiden) and "Heidenröslein" (Wild Rose)

Franz Schubert (text by Claudius and by Goethe)

Franz Schubert (1797–1828) was a masterful composer of symphonies, sonatas, and string quartets, but is perhaps best known for his *Lieder* (songs), of which he wrote more than six hundred. "Death and the Maiden" is a dialogue between a young woman who pleads for her life and the figure of Death, who claims her, promising that she will sleep softly in his arms. "Heidenröslein" is a simple, seemingly artless depiction of a boy admiring a flower.

Der Tod und das Mädchen
(Death and the Maiden)

Franz Schubert

Text by Claudius

Das erste Zeitmaß. (*The first tempo.*)
Der Tod. (Death)

Gib dei-ne Hand, du schön und zart Ge - bild! bin Freund und kom-me nicht zu __ stra - fen. Sei gut-es Muts! ich, bin nicht wild, sollst sanft in mei-nen Ar-men schla - fen!

Vorüber, ach, vorüber!
geh, wilder Knochenmann!
Ich bin noch jung, geh, Lieber!
und rühre mich nicht an,
und rühre mich nicht an.
Gib deine Hand, du schön und zart Gebild!
bin Freund und komme nicht zu strafen.
Sei gutes Muts! ich, bin nicht wild,
sollst sanft in meinen Armen schlafen!

Pass by, ah, pass by!
Go, harsh, bony Death!
I am still young, go, my dear!
and do not touch me,
and do not touch me.
Give me your hand, you beautiful, sweet creature!
I am a friend and do not come to punish.
Have courage! I am not cruel.
Softly in my arms you will sleep!

Heidenröslein (Wild Rose)

Franz Schubert

Text by Goethe

Sah ein Knab' ein Röslein stehn, Röslein auf der Heiden,
war so jung und morgenschön,
lief er schnell es nah' zu sehn, sah's mit vielen Freuden.
Röslein, Röslein, Röslein roth, Röslein auf der Heiden.

A boy saw a wild rose, a wild rose amid the heather,
it was so fresh and beautiful
he ran quickly to gaze at it, gaze with great joy.
Little rose, little red rose, rose amid the heather.

"Wenn ich in deine Augen seh'" (When I Look into Your Eyes), from *Dichterliebe (A Poet's Love)*

Robert Schumann (text by Heinrich Heine)

Robert Schumann (1810–56) wrote several song cycles (collections of songs with interrelated texts). *Dichterliebe (A Poet's Love)*, written in 1840 to poems by the famous German poet Heinrich Heine, is probably the best known of these. The fourth song, "Wenn ich in deine Augen seh'" (When I Look into Your Eyes), sets a deceptively simple two-stanza poem that seems at first to be a gentle love lyric, but ends with a surprising ironic twist.

Wenn ich in deine Augen seh'
(When I Look into Your Eyes)

Robert Schumann

Text by Heinrich Heine

Lyrics in the music:

Wenn ich in dei - ne Au - gen seh', so schwin-det all' mein Leid und Weh; doch wenn ich küs - se dei - nen Mund, so werd' ich ganz und gar - ge - sund. Wenn ich mich lehn' an dei - ne Brust, kommt's ü - ber mich wie Him - mels

(continued)

Wenn ich in deine Augen seh',
so schwindet all' mein Leid und Weh;
doch wenn ich küsse deinen Mund,
so werd' ich ganz und gargesund.
Wenn ich mich lehn' an deine Brust,
kommt's über mich wie Himmels lust;
doch wenn du sprichst: "Ich liebe dich!"
so muss ich weinen bitterlich.

When I into your eyes look,
then fades all my pain and sorrow.
and when I kiss your lips,
then I become entirely well.
When I rest upon your breast,
comes over me a heavenly bliss;
but when you say: "I love you!"
then must I weep bitterly.

Glossary

Accent. A particular emphasis on a *pitch*, either by playing it louder, higher, or longer than surrounding pitches, or by positioning it on a strong part of the *measure*, such as the *downbeat* (Lesson 6).

Accent mark. A notational symbol (>) indicating that a note is to be stressed in some way, often by being played more loudly (Lesson 13).

Accidentals. Symbols placed before *notes* that raise them (*sharp sign*, ♯) or lower them (*flat sign*, ♭) by one *semitone* (Lesson 3). See also *double sharp* and *double flat*, which respectively raise or lower a pitch by two semitones.

Alla breve. A *time signature* notated as ¢ where the *measure* contains two *half-note beats* (Lesson 10).

Alto. The second-highest note in a chord or the second-highest-sounding melodic line (Lesson 32).

Alto clef. See *clef*.

Anacrusis. An incomplete preliminary measure (also called a *pickup* or *upbeat*) (Lesson 8).

Antecedent phrase. The first *phrase* in a *parallel period*, ending with a *half cadence* on the *dominant harmony* (Lesson 35).

Arpeggiation. Playing the notes of a *triad* or *seventh chord* consecutively rather than simultaneously (Lesson 27).

Ascending melodic minor. See *melodic minor*.

Augmentation dot. A notational symbol placed directly after a note that increases the time-value of the note by one-half. For example, a dotted *half note* has the value of a half note plus a *quarter note*; a dotted quarter note has the value of a quarter note plus an *eighth note*; a dotted eighth note has the value of an eighth note plus a *sixteenth note* (Lesson 8).

Augmented triad. A triad that consists of a major third and an augmented fifth above its *root* (Lesson 27).

Authentic cadence. A *progression* from *dominant* to *tonic* that occurs at the end of a *phrase* and provides a strong sense of arrival on the tonic (Lesson 35).

Bar. See *measure*.

Barline. A vertical line through the *staff* that divides it into *measures* (or *bars*).

Bass. The lowest-sounding note in a chord, or the lowest-sounding melodic line (Lessons 28 and 32).

Bass clef. See *clef*.

Beam. A horizontal line that connects notational *stems* to create groupings of two or four *eighth* or *sixteenth notes* (*double beam*) (Lesson 7).

Beat. A steady, regular rhythmic pulsation (Lesson 6).

Cadence. A musical punctuation point that conveys a sense of harmonic arrival, such as an *authentic cadence*, a *half cadence*, or a *plagal cadence* (Lesson 35).

Chord inversion. The positioning of the third or fifth of a triad, or the third, fifth, or seventh of a seventh chord, in the bass (Lessons 28 and 31).

Chord symbols. Names for *triads* and *seventh chords* that designate their *root* with a letter name and their quality and position with additional symbols (Lessons 27 and 28).

Circle of fifths. The arrangement of the twelve notes into a series of ascending perfect fifths, returning to its starting point after all twelve notes have been traversed (Lessons 15, 16, and 19).

Clef. A symbol placed at the beginning of a *staff* to identify locations on the staff with specific pitches (Lesson 3). The most commonly used clefs are the *treble clef*, also known as the *G-clef*, which assigns the G above middle C to the second line of the staff, and the *bass clef*, also known as the *F-clef*, which assigns the F below middle C to the fourth line of the staff (Lessons 3 and 4). Less common are *alto clef* (assigns middle C to the middle line of the staff) and *tenor clef* (which assigns middle C to the fourth line of the staff) (Chapter 1: Supplementary Lesson).

Common time. Another designation for $\frac{4}{4}$ *meter*, referred to with the *time signature* 𝄴 (Lesson 6).

Compound interval. An *interval* larger than an *octave*, such as a ninth (compound second), tenth (compound third), or eleventh (compound fourth) (Lesson 21).

Compound meter. A *meter* in which the *beat* is divided into three parts and the beat itself is a *dotted note*. The most common compound meter is $\frac{6}{8}$, where the beat is a dotted quarter note (Lesson 12).

Consequent phrase. The second *phrase* in a *parallel period*, ending with an *authentic cadence* on the *tonic harmony* (Lesson 35).

Consonance. The quality of *intervals* and *chords* as relatively harmonious, blended, and stable (compared to *dissonance*) (Lesson 25).

Descending melodic minor. See *melodic minor*.

Diminished triad. A *triad* that consists of a minor third and a diminished fifth above its *root* (Lesson 27).

Dissonance. The quality of *intervals* and *chords* as relatively inharmonious, unblended, and unstable (compared to *consonance*) (Lesson 25).

Dominant. A name for *scale-degree* $\hat{5}$ or for the triad built on that degree (Lessons 14, 29, and 32).

Dominant preparation chord. A chord that precedes and leads to the dominant. Also called a *predominant chord* (Lesson 34).

Dominant seventh chord. A *seventh chord* that consists of a major *triad* and a minor seventh (or a major triad with a minor third added on top). Also called a *major-minor seventh chord* (Lessons 31 and 32).

Dot. See *augmentation dot*.

Dotted note. See *augmentation dot*.

Double beam. See *beam*.

Double flag. See *flag*.

Double flat. An *accidental* ♭♭ that lowers the *pitch* of a *note* by two *semitones* (Chapter 1: Supplementary Lesson).

Double sharp. An *accidental* x that raises the *pitch* of a *note* by two *semitones* (Chapter 1: Supplementary Lesson).

469

Doubling. Representing one part of a chord (*root*, third, fifth, or seventh) with two or more different notes, a unison or octave apart (Lesson 27). In certain situations, composers may prefer certain doublings and avoid others (Lesson 32 and Chapter 6: Supplementary Lesson).

Downbeat. The first *beat* of a *measure*, which typically receives a sense of weight or accent (Lessons 6 and 10).

Duple meter. A *meter* involving two *beats* per *measure*. Common examples are $\frac{2}{4}$ and $\frac{2}{2}$ (Lessons 10 and 11).

Eighth note. A duration equivalent to one-half of a *quarter note*. Written with a filled-in *notehead* and a *stem* with a *flag*. When two eighth notes occur together in a pair, it is customary to dispense with the flags and join them with a *beam* (Lesson 7).

Embellishing tones. Tones (including *passing tones* and *neighboring tones*) used to decorate tones that belong to a stable harmony. Also called *nonharmonic tones* (Lesson 33).

Enharmonic equivalents. Two different names for the same *pitch* (e.g., C♯ and D♭), *scale* (e.g., F♯ major and G♭ major), or *interval* (e.g., C–D♯ and C–E♭) (Lessons 3, 15, and 22).

F-clef. See *clef*.

Figured bass. Numbers that identify the *intervals* formed above a *bass* note (Lesson 28).

First inversion. The position of a chord in which the third of a triad or seventh chord is in the bass (Lessons 28 and 31).

Flag. A notational symbol attached to a *stem* to turn a *quarter note* into an *eighth note*. A double flag identifies a *sixteenth note* (Lesson 7).

Flat sign (♭). An *accidental* placed before a *note* that lowers its *pitch* by one *semitone* (Lesson 3).

G-clef. See *clef*.

Grand staff. See *Great staff*.

Great staff. A combination of two staves connected by a brace, the upper with a *treble clef* and the lower with a *bass clef*. Also called a *grand staff* (Lesson 5).

Half cadence. An arrival on the *dominant* at the end of a *phrase* (Lesson 35).

Half note. A duration equivalent to two *quarter notes*, written as an open *notehead* with a *stem* (Lesson 6).

Half step. The smaller of two sizes of *step* (*whole step* is the other). A half step is the distance between two adjacent white keys of the piano where there is no black key between them (i.e., E–F and B–C) (Lesson 2). More generally, a half step is the smallest musical interval formed between any adjacent keys, white or black. Also called a *semitone*.

Harmonic intervals. *Intervals* comprised of notes sounding at the same time (Lesson 21).

Harmonic minor. A variant form of the minor scale in which scale-degree 7 is raised one *semitone* from its position in the *natural minor* (Lesson 20).

Interval. The distance between two notes, measured in terms of *interval size* and *interval quality* (Lesson 21).

Interval inversion. An *interval* is inverted by reversing the registral order of its upper and lower notes (bottom becomes top and top becomes bottom). An *octave* may be divided into two intervals related by inversion; conversely, an interval can be combined with its inversion to make up an octave (Lesson 23).

Interval quality. Variation among intervals of the same numerical size depending on the number of semitones they contain. Intervals may be *diminished*, *minor*, *perfect*, *major*, or *augmented* in quality (Lesson 22).

Interval size. The number of steps the interval contains (or the number of different letter names it spans), disregarding any accidentals (Lesson 21).

Inversion. See *interval inversion* or *chord inversion*.

Key. (1) One of the eighty-eight visible levers comprising a *keyboard* that a pianist depresses to produce musical sounds (Lesson 2). (2) The network of pitch relationships that defines one note as a *tonic* and assigns subordinate functions to the other notes (Lessons 16 and 19).

Keyboard. The set of *keys* that the player of a piano (or other keyboard instrument) depresses to produce musical sounds. The typical piano keyboard contains eighty-eight keys, some white and some black, each producing a different *pitch* (Lesson 2).

Keyboard style. An arrangement of harmonies on the *great staff* with three *voices* (*soprano*, *alto*, and *tenor*) in the *treble clef* and one (*bass*) in the *bass clef* (Lesson 32).

Key signature. An arrangement of sharps or flats at the beginning of the staff that defines the major or minor scale in use (Lesson 16).

Leading tone. A name for *scale-degree* 7 in major or for the triad built on that degree (Lessons 14 and 29). Similarly for scale-degree 7 in minor, when it is raised one *semitone* from its natural position to a position one semitone below the *tonic* (Lessons 17 and 30).

Leap. One of two kinds of melodic motion (*step* is the other). A leap is any motion bigger than a step (Lesson 1).

Ledger lines. Short lines parallel to the lines of the *staff* that function to extend the staff either up or down (Lesson 1).

Letter name. The way every pitch is identified by one of the first seven letters of the alphabet—A, B, C, D, E, F, G—either alone or modified by an *accidental* (*sharp* or *flat*) (Lesson 2).

Major-minor seventh chord. A *seventh chord* that consists of a major *triad* and a minor seventh (or a major triad with a minor third added on top). Also called a *dominant seventh chord* (Lesson 31).

Major scale. A *scale* written above any given note that follows a particular sequence of *whole tones* (WT) and *semitones* (ST): WT–WT–ST–WT–WT–WT–ST (Lesson 14).

Major triad. A triad that consists of a major third and a perfect fifth above its root (Lesson 27).

Measure. A fixed grouping of beats. Common measure lengths are two, three, or four *quarter notes* in duration. Measures are also called *bars* (Lesson 6).

Mediant. A name for *scale-degree* 3 or for the triad built on that degree (Lessons 14 and 29).

Melodic intervals. *Intervals* comprised of notes sounding one at a time in succession, either ascending or descending in motion (Lesson 21).

Melodic minor. A variant of the minor scale which, in its *ascending* form, raises both scale-degrees 6 and 7 from their positions in the *natural minor*. Its *descending* form is identical to the natural minor (Lesson 20).

Meter. A fixed, recurring arrangement of *beats* in a *measure* (Lesson 6).

Middle C. The pitch C located in the middle of the piano *keyboard*, on the first line below the *treble staff*, and on the first line above the *bass staff* (Lessons 2, 3, and 4). According to common systems of *octave designation*, middle C is either C4 or c1 (Chapter 1: Supplementary Lesson).

Minor scale. A *scale* written above any given note that follows a particular sequence of *whole tones* (WT) and *semitones* (ST): WT–ST–WT–WT–ST– WT–WT (Lesson 17).

Minor triad. A *triad* that consists of a minor third and a perfect fifth above its *root* (Lesson 27).

Natural interval. An *interval* formed between *notes* without any *accidentals* (sharps or flats) (Lesson 22).

Natural minor. The minor scale that corresponds to the key signature, without any alteration of scale-degrees 6̂ or 7̂ (Lesson 20).

Natural seventh chords. The seven *seventh chords* formed from notes without any *accidentals* (sharps or flats): C–E–G–B, D–F–A–C, E–G–B–D, F–A–C–E, G–B–D–F, A–C–E–G, B–D–F–A (Chapter 5: Supplementary Lesson).

Natural sign. An *accidental* placed before a *note* that undoes the effect of a previous *sharp* or *flat sign*, restoring the note to its original, unaltered *pitch* (Lesson 3).

Natural triads. The seven *triads* formed from notes without any *accidentals* (sharps or flats): C–E–G, D–F–A, E–G–B, F–A–C, G–B–D, A–C–E, and B–D–F (Lesson 27).

Neighboring chord. A chord used to embellish a more stable chord by harmonizing a neighboring note in the bass or soprano (Lesson 33).

Neighboring tone. An *embellishing tone* that moves by step away from and back to a harmony tone (Lesson 33).

Nonharmonic tones. See *embellishing tones*.

Note. A symbol used in music notation to represent the duration and *pitch* of a sound (Lesson 1). More casually, the term *note* is used throughout this book to refer to any musical sound or tone.

Notehead. An open or filled-in oval that specifies where on the *staff* a *note* is to occur (Lesson 1).

Octave. The *interval* between two notes with the same letter name (Lesson 2).

Octave designation. A way of assigning a *pitch* to a particular *octave* by attaching a number to its letter name. *Middle C*, for example, is designated C4, and all of the notes above it, but lower than the next higher C (C5), also lie in the 4-octave (Chapter 1: Supplementary Lesson).

Octave sign. A text symbol (*8va* or *8vb*) used to indicate that *notes* should be played one *octave* higher or lower than written (Chapter 1: Supplementary Lesson).

Parallel keys. Major and minor scales that share the same tonic. For example, D major is the *parallel major* of D minor, and D minor is the *parallel minor* of D major (Lesson 19).

Parallel period. A combination of *antecedent* and *consequent* *phrases* (Lesson 35).

Passing chord. A chord used to connect two more stable chords by harmonizing a passing tone in the bass (Lesson 33).

Passing tone. An embellishing tone that fills in the space between two harmony tones that lie the interval of a third apart (Lesson 33).

Period. A longer *phrase* that contains at least two shorter ones (Lesson 35).

Phrase. A self-contained group of *measures* that ends with a *cadence* (Lesson 35).

Pickup. See *anacrusis*.

Pitch. A musical sound at some particular point along the continuum from the lowest to the highest audible sound. Each of the eighty-eight keys of the piano keyboard represents a distinct pitch (Lessons 1 and 2).

Plagal cadence. A progression from *subdominant* to *tonic* at the end of a *phrase*, usually occurring after an *authentic cadence* as an extra confirmation (Lesson 35).

Predominant chord. See *dominant preparation chord*.

Progression. A succession of harmonies in which each leads purposefully to the next (Lesson 32).

Prolongation. The extension in time of a harmony through the use of *embellishing tones* (including *passing tones* and *neighboring tones*) (Lesson 33).

Quadruple meter. A *meter* involving four *beats* per *measure*. The most common example is $\frac{4}{4}$ (Lesson 11).

Quarter note. The most common unit of musical duration, written with a filled-in *notehead* and a *stem* (Lesson 6).

Relative keys. Major and minor scales that share the same key signature. For example, F major is the *relative major* of D minor, and D minor is the *relative minor* of F major (Lesson 19).

Rest. A silence of a specified duration (Lesson 9).

Rhythm. A measure of musical activity in time, including particularly duration (Lesson 6).

Roman numerals. A nomenclature for identifying the *roots* of *triads* or *seventh chords* according to their *scale-degree* (Lessons 29 and 30).

Root. The fundamental, generating tone of a *triad* or *seventh chord*. When the harmony is written in the closest possible stack of thirds, the root will be the lowest note (Lesson 27).

Root position. The position of a *triad* or *seventh* chord in which the *root* is in the *bass* (Lesson 28).

Scale. A collection of notes used in a musical composition and customarily written in ascending order within an *octave* (Lesson 14).

Scale degree. The order position of each note within a scale: the first note of the scale is the first degree; the second note is the second degree; and so on (Lessons 14 and 17).

Scale-degree name. Each degree of the *scale* is identified by a customary name: 1̂ = *tonic*; 2̂ = *supertonic*; 3̂ = *mediant*; 4̂ = *subdominant*; 5̂ = *dominant*; 6̂ = *submediant*; 7 in major = *leading tone*; 7 in minor = *subtonic* or *leading tone* (Lessons 14 and 17).

Scale-degree number. Each degree of the scale is assigned an ordinal number, usually written with a caret over it (Lessons 14 and 17).

Second inversion. The position of a chord in which the fifth of a triad or seventh chord is in the bass (Lessons 28 and 31).

Semitone. The smallest musical distance, equivalent to the *interval* between any two adjacent *keys* (black or white) on the *keyboard* (Lessons 3 and 14). Also called a *half step*.

Seventh chord. A *triad* plus the *interval* of a seventh over a shared *root* (or a triad plus an additional third on top) (Lesson 31).

Sharp sign (♯). An *accidental* placed before a *note* that lowers its *pitch* by one semitone (Lesson 3).

Simple interval. An interval smaller than an octave (e.g., a second, third, fourth, fifth, sixth, or seventh) (Lesson 21).

Simple meter. A *meter* in which the *beat* is divided into two parts. In $\frac{4}{4}$, for example, the quarter-note beat is divided into two eighth notes (Lesson 12).

Sixteenth note. A duration equivalent to one-half of an *eighth note* or one-quarter of a *quarter note*. Written with a filled-in *notehead* and a *stem* with a double *flag*. When four sixteenth notes occur together as a group, it is customary to dispense with the flags and join them with a double *beam* (Lesson 7).

Sixty-fourth note. A duration equivalent to one-half of a thirty-second note or one-quarter of a *sixteenth note*. Written with a filled-in *notehead* and a *stem* with a quadruple *flag* or *beam* (Chapter 2: Supplementary Lesson).

Slur. A curved line that connects two notes of a different *pitch*, and indicates that they are to be smoothly connected in performance (not to be confused with a *tie*, which connects and combines two notes of the same pitch) (Lesson 8).

Solfège syllables. Syllables (do, re, mi, fa, sol, la, ti) used to name *scale degrees* when music is sung (Lessons 14 and 17).

Soprano. The highest note in a chord or the highest-sounding melodic line (Lessons 28 and 32).

Staff. Five parallel lines separated by four spaces. Music is written by positioning *notes* on the lines or in the spaces (Lesson 1).

Stem. A vertical line that extends up or down from a *notehead*, used to define particular durations (Lesson 6).

Step. One of two kinds of melodic motion (*leap* is the other). As represented on the *staff*, a step involves motion from a line up or down to an adjacent space, or from a space up or down to an adjacent line (Lesson 1).

Subdominant. A name for *scale-degree* $\hat{4}$ or for the triad built on that degree (Lessons 14 and 29).

Submediant. A name for *scale-degree* $\hat{6}$ or for the triad built on that degree (Lessons 14 and 29).

Subtonic. A name for *scale-degree* $\hat{7}$ in minor—a *whole tone* below the *tonic*—or for the triad built on that degree (Lessons 17 and 30).

Supertonic. A name for *scale-degree* $\hat{2}$ or for the triad built on that degree (Lessons 14 and 29).

Syncopation. The contradiction of a metrical pattern that results in strong beats made weak and weak beats made strong (Lesson 13).

Tempo. The speed of the *beats*, customarily indicated either with a one-word character description or with the number of beats per minute (Lesson 6).

Tenor. The second-lowest note in a chord or the second-lowest-sounding melodic line (Lesson 32).

Tenor clef. See *clef*.

Third inversion. The position of a chord in which the seventh of a seventh chord is in the bass (Lesson 31).

Thirty-second note. A duration equivalent to one-half of a *sixteenth note* or one-quarter of an *eighth note*. Written with a filled-in *notehead* and a *stem* with a triple *flag* or *beam* (Chapter 2: Supplementary Lesson).

Tie. A curved line that connects two notes of the same *pitch* (not to be confused with a *slur*, which connects two notes of different pitch). The tie combines those two notes into a single note whose duration is the sum of the two notes (Lessons 8 and 13).

Time signature. A pair of vertically aligned numbers placed at the beginning of the *staff* to indicate which note value is acting as the *beat* and how many beats there are in the *measure*. Common time signatures are $\frac{4}{4}$, $\frac{2}{4}$, and $\frac{3}{4}$. The number at the bottom indicates which note value is acting as the beat (4 indicates a quarter note) and the number at the top indicates the number of beats per measure (Lesson 6).

Tonic. A name for *scale-degree* $\hat{1}$ or for the triad built on that degree (Lessons 14, 29, and 32).

Transposition. Rewriting a *scale*, melody, passage, or piece at a different *pitch* level (Lessons 15 and 18).

Treble clef. See *clef*.

Triad. The basic harmony of tonal music, consisting of three notes: a fifth divided into two thirds. There are four different qualities of triad: *diminished*, *minor*, *major*, and *augmented*. Triads consist of a *root*, a *third*, and a *fifth* (Lesson 27).

Triple meter. A *meter* involving three *beats* per *measure*. The most common example is $\frac{3}{4}$ (Lesson 11).

Triplet. A rhythmic value that divides into three parts a note that is normally divided in two. A quarter note, for example, is usually divided into two eighth notes, but can be divided instead into an eighth-note triplet (Chapter 2: Supplementary Lesson).

Tritone. Name sometimes given to the interval of the augmented fourth, because it spans three whole tones (Lesson 24).

Upbeat. The last *beat* in a *measure* which, although weak in relation to the *downbeat*, nonetheless gives a sense of directed, dynamic motion toward the downbeat (Lessons 6 and 10).

Voices. The distinct registral lines that move through a *progression* of harmonies: *soprano*, *alto*, *tenor*, and *bass* (Lesson 32).

Voice leading. The movement of *voices* from chord to chord within a *progression* of harmonies (Chapter 6: Supplementary Lesson).

Whole note. A duration equivalent to two *half notes* or four *quarter notes*, written as an open *notehead* with no *stem* (Lesson 6).

Whole step. The larger of two different sizes of *step* (*half step* is the other). A whole step is the distance between two adjacent white keys of the piano where there is no black key between them (i.e., C–D, D–E, F–G, G–A, and A–B) (Lesson 2). A whole step consists of two half steps. Also called a *whole tone*.

Whole tone. An *interval* comprised of two semitones (Lesson 14). Also called a *whole step*.